DATA COMMUNICATIONS

To the three Js:

Jilly, Jo-Jo and Jasper

DATA COMMUNICATIONS
An Introductory Guide

David L.Hebditch

Elek Science

London

First Published in Great Britain in 1975 by
Paul Elek (Scientific Books) Ltd.,
54-58 Caledonian Road,
London N1 9RN

ISBN 0 236 31098 4

Printed in Great Britain by Unwin Brothers Limited,
The Gresham Press, Old Woking, Surrey, England
A member of the Staples Printing Group

CONTENTS

INTRODUCTION

This book has been written for data processing professionals with batch experience who are about to get involved in the field of data communications. Students for the British Computer Society examinations will find that much of the Part I syllabus is covered.

The author is not a telecommunications engineer and only enough detail has been included to give computer people adequate background knowledge for progression to learning practical techniques in the design and implementation of online systems.

I would like to thank Mr. R.D. Bright, Mr. W.A.F. Barbour, Mr. J.A. Lockwood, Mr. M.J. Burgess (all of Post Office Data Communications Marketing), Mr. T.J. Knappett (of Post Office Network Planning Department) and Mr. S.R.V. Paramor (of Post Office External Telecommunications Executive) for reading Chapter 10 and putting me right on many points of detail. I must, however, bear responsibility for the final version (especially the opinions!).

In addition, I would like to express my gratitude to my colleagues at Pliener Associates Limited for their criticisms, suggestions and support. The various typescripts were diligently produced by Jill Wilson and Jane Taylor who were very patient in dealing with the usual last-minute changes.

Finally, I should thank the many companies who kindly contributed photographs and Allan Pliener for permission to use Pliener Associates' Letraset in the Illustrations.

CHAPTER 1

TELECOMMUNICATIONS BACKGROUND

1.1 TRANSMISSION SYSTEMS

A good point at which to start a book on data communications might
be to look at the general structure of any kind of system involving
transmission. The three primary components of a system are shown in
Figure 1.1. The source is the point of origination, the medium is
the means by which the transmission takes place and the sink is at
the end of the transfer. In a simple teleprocessing system the source
might be a terminal keyboard, the medium a telephone line and the sink
a computer. It will be obvious that sources may also be sinks and sinks
may also be sources, (perhaps at the same time) in all types of transmission systems.

Figure 1.1. Elements of a transmission system

As we are mainly interested in the transmission of data, the medium
within a computer room might be the processor's input-output channels
and for external connections telephone or telegraph lines. For data
transmission particularly, Figure 1.1 would be redrawn, as in Figure 1.2,

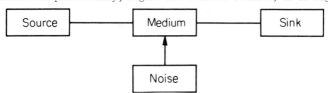

Figure 1.2. Elements of a data transmission system

to show another non-physical component 'noise'. Although 'noise' is not
a physical component of the system it assumes a very high degree of importance in data communications. Noise usually consists of unpredicted

1

(and unwanted) electrical impulses, crosstalk and brief circuit breaks
which cause loss of data and influence the speed at which it can be
transmitted. The problems of noise and how it is handled in more detail
will be dealt with in Chapter 3.

1.2   TELECOMMUNICATIONS OVERVIEW

In terms of age, telecommunications is an older technology to that
of computers. It was developed to fulfil a need firstly for the transmission of messages (telegraph) and subsequently for the transmission
of the human voice (telephone). Computers came on the scene much later
and one could speculate on how our telecommunications networks might have
developed in the unlikely situation of computers being around in Bell's
time. However, we are looking through the wrong end of the telescope;
we have to use the networks described below because, at the time of
writing, they are all that are available.

There are presently two functionally different networks in use,

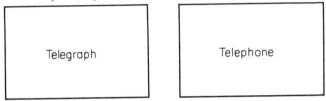

Figure 1.3.   Telecommunications networks

telegraph and telephone (Figure 1.3). From the view point of data
transmission, these may each be further divided into 'leased','dedicated'
or 'private' and 'switched' networks (Figure 1.4). Dedicated circuits
are those allocated to one customer for his own use full-time (and sometimes part-time). This might be used where there is a high volume of
messages between, say, a company's factory in Glasgow and its Head
Office in London. If the messages were to be printed they might use
a (leased) telegraph line; if spoken, a leased telephone line (sometimes
called a 'tie line'). Such dedicated lines are also used to link automatic fire alarms to the local Fire Station, burglar alarms to the Police
Station or a typewriter to a computer.

In actual fact, of course, dedicated circuits are the same lines as
used for switched connections but made unavailable to dialling because
they are branched past the switchgear in the exchanges. However, the
switched networks are invariably more extensive than dedicated circuits;
a telephone which can potentially be connected to any other is generally
much more useful than a handset connected to just one other phone. The

2

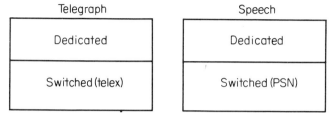

Figure 1.4. Telecommunication network: switched and dedicated lines

normal telephone system is variously referred to as the 'Public Switched Network', 'Switched Public Network' or the 'Public Switched Telephone Network' (PSN, SPN, PSTN).

There is also a switched service for teleprinters which is known in the U.K. as Telex. Figures 1.5 and 1.6 show some aspects of the two networks in more detail.

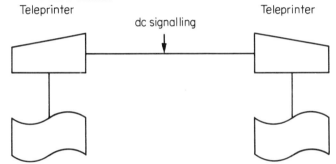

Figure 1.5. Telegraph communications. Maximum speed of 110 bits/sec on leased circuits and a dial-up service known as Telex with a speed of 50 bits/sec (6·6 ch/sec). Paper tape facilities are available at each end (messages can be prepunched for faster transmission via the tape reader). There are 20,000 connections in the U.K. and it has international use including TELEX

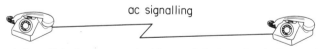

Figure 1.6. Telephone communications. Telephone handset or private exchange plus extensions) at each end. Speeds up to and over 9600 bits/sec on leased circuits and 1200 bits/sec (sometimes 4800 bits/sec) on public switched network (PSN). There are 8 million plus connections in the U.K. and wide international use (including PSN)

The networks have been described as being functionally different, but in practice the Post Office transmits telegraph data over the voice network for reasons of economy. This does not affect the user in any way. Practical aspects of the use of the telegraph and telephone networks for data transmission in the U.K. and Europe are described more fully in Chapter 10.

The use of data transmission is growing rapidly; there are over 30,000 terminals presently installed in the U.K. and this is expected to reach more than a quarter of a million by the end of the 1970s. In the U.S.A. it is estimated that more information is being transmitted on their telephone network by computers than by the human voice. In recognition of these important trends, the Post Office is developing a digital data service (DDS) primarily for use by computers. Users will be able to switch circuits and also 'post' packages of data which will be 'delivered' to their destinations after a short delay. Should this development proceed successfully Figure 1.4 could be redrawn as in Figure 1.7 to show a third network for data. However, it seems likely that the telegraph network will become an integral part of the data network and even the distinction between the speech and data networks will become less well defined as speech is digitised (using a technique known as pulse code modulation) and switched through computer-controlled exchanges.

Unfortunately, all this is very much for the future; it is unlikely that the data network will be installed to any great extent, before the 1980s. However, in 1975 the Post Office* is due to launch EPSS, the 'Experimental Packet Switching Service'. This system is a precursor to DDS and is described in more detail in Chapter 10.

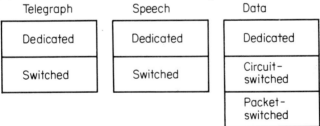

Figure 1.7.   U.K. telecommunications network after the introduction of the Digital Data Network (DDN)

---

* Throughout this book the generally recognised abbreviation 'PTT' is used to indicate the 'Posts, Telegraph and Telephone' authority or the 'Recognised Private Operating Agency' of any country. When the term 'Post Office' is used it means the RPOA of the U.K.

Quite significant developments are taking place within the scope of the present system. Simple pairs of wires are now only used at the very ends of circuits and new developments include the use of satellites, micro-wave links, waveguides and even lasers to improve the speed and reliability of transmission. James Martin's excellent book *'Telecommunications and the Computer'* discusses the past, present and future of the technology in great detail and is recommended reading for those wishing to establish a deeper knowledge of the subject.

QUESTIONS, DISCUSSION TOPICS AND ASSIGNMENTS

1. Specify the source, medium and sink of at least five information transmission systems. In each case indicate the 'noise' that might occur.

2. Using whatever sources are available to you draw a chart plotting the history of the development of telecommunications. Comment on the contributions made by:

> Alexander Bell,
> Marconi,
> Strowger and
> Morse.

3. Consider some of the circumstances under which telephone and telegraph lines might be leased full-time rather than dialled as required.

4. Investigate the extent of public telephone networks in each EEC country and the United States. Draw a histogram of the ratios of telephones installed per head of population.

5

CHAPTER 2
HOW COMPUTERS USE TELEGRAPH CIRCUITS

You will have noticed from the previous chapter that the major difference between telegraph and telephone lines is that telegraph circuits are designed for *digital* transmission whereas telephone lines are designed for *analogue* transmission.

2.1 DIGITAL TRANSMISSION

In view of the fact that computer devices are themselves digital by nature it would seem that the telegraph network is the most obvious choice for data transmission. Certainly the interface would be easy to implement; all that is required is some means of converting between the computer signal levels of +6 V and -6 V to +80 V and -80 V which is the most common standard for telegraph transmission (Figure 2.1).

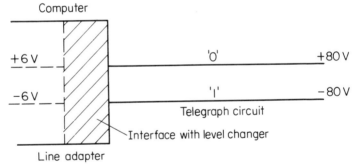

Figure 2.1. The interface between a computer device and a telegraph circuit

2.2 SPEED LIMITATIONS

Why then, does most data transmission take place on telephone lines? The objection to the public telegraph system is the maximum speed of 110 bits/sec. (200 bits/sec in some continental European countries). This maximum is impossible for two reasons; the type of input/output devices for which the network was designed did not require a higher speed and the cost of universally increasing the capacity would be prohibitive.

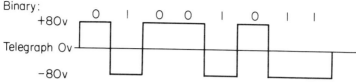

Figure 2.2.   Telegraph transmission

Let us examine the problem in more detail. Figure 2.2 shows the binary value '01001011' as it might be transmitted down a telegraph line. However, the pattern will not travel an unlimited distance down the line whilst retaining its original shape exactly. Data transmission would be very simple if that were the case. In fact, much of the power of the original signal is lost and the shape increasingly distorted the further it travels until it might look something like Figure 2.3. Here

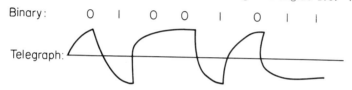

Figure 2.3.   Telegraph distortion

it will be seen that the bit pattern is still quite recognisable. But if the speed of transmission is changed, that is the rate at which the voltage is changed, the signal becomes more and more incoherent (is it not the same with human speech?). Figure 2.4 illustrates this effect.

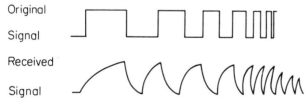

Figure 2.4.   Effect of distortion according to the speed of the pulse rate

Dictortion should not be confused with *noise*. The former is a totally calculable characteristic of the channel whereas the latter is of a random nature and only predictable in statistical terms. Noise is more of a problem on telephone lines (*see* Chapter 3 for a more detailed explanation of both distortion and noise).

7

2.3   REPEATERS

The way in which this problem is overcome in the telegraph system (which works world-wide, of course) is through the use of devices known as *regenerative repeaters*. Repeaters are fitted into a circuit at the furthest point at which they can still recognise, with a high degree of accuracy, the pulse train being transmitted. The repeater then regenerates each bit of the signal at its original strength (Figure 2.5).

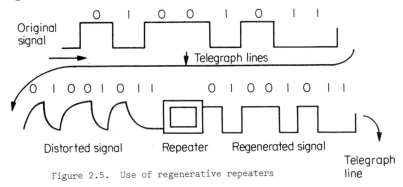

Figure 2.5.   Use of regenerative repeaters

Telegraph networks were designed to operate at a maximum speed of 110 bits/sec; very slow in computer terms. This speed is determined by the positioning of the repeaters (or rather the speed determines the location of the repeaters) and to increase this maximum by even a small degree to, say 500 bits/sec., would involve the addition of an enormous number of repeaters. Although the devices are relatively inexpensive, the logistics of the operation would be prohibitive even on a national basis. Also the end result, a 500 bits/sec service, would be of no benefit to existing teleprinter users unless they changed their equipment and would be of limited benefit to those wishing to transmit data. However, some teleprocessing systems make use of telegraph (or *baseband*) transmission for short local circuits which do not need to use lines provided by the PTT. Depending upon the distance the data is being transmitted, it is often possible to achieve reliability at speeds up to 9600 bits/sec.

QUESTIONS, DISCUSSION TOPICS AND ASSIGNMENTS

1. Contact a manufacturer who supplies a device for baseband transmission. Draw a graph showing the relationship between reliable transmission speed and the length of the circuit being used.

2. Discuss the benefits and limitations of using the Telex service

for the transmission of data to a computer centre on an off-line basis (i.e. teleprinter to teleprinter) using paper tape at least at the receiving end.

CHAPTER 3
CHARACTERISTICS OF TELEPHONE LINES

The first (perhaps obvious) point to note about telephone lines is
that they were not designed for the transmission of data by anything
other than the human voice. Indeed, the reasons why the telephone
network is used are that it is already installed and available and
that it provides very extensive coverage of the whole country having
over 8 million connections in the U.K. alone. Because the very nature
of the telephone network imposes constraints on the ways in which data
can be transmitted, it is important to understand the main characteristics
of speech circuits.

3.1 SPEECH TRANSMISSION

The principle of speech transmission is that the microphone in a
telephone handset produces on the lines an electrical analogy of the
soundwaves it receives and the speaker components (including the one
in the handset of the person talking) translate the signals back into
sounds. Figure 3.1 illustrates the main characteristics of a regular
waveform. The frequency may be thought of as 'pitch' and amplitude as
'loudness'. Three other terms which we shall use are *bandwidth*, *passband*
and *cutoff frequencies*.

Bandwidth is used to indicate the width of a range of frequencies.
Therefore, if a particular communications channel can accommodate
frequencies between 1900 Hz and 2100 Hz its bandwidth is 200 Hz.
(2100 - 1900).

A *passband* is a particular slot in the frequency spectrum. The
passband of the 200 Hz bandwidth channel mentioned above is 1900 - 2100 Hz
and there might be another 200 Hz channel at a passband of 1200 - 1400 Hz.

Cutoff frequencies are the upper and lower limits of a particular
passband. The passbands described above have cutoffs at 1200 Hz, 1400 Hz,
1900 Hz and 2100 Hz. (*see* Figure 4.25)

10

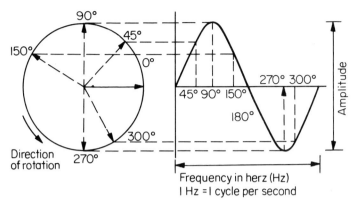

Figure 3.1.   Characteristics of a simple waveform. The phase is
represented by a rotating vector. One 360 degree
rotation is equivalent to one cycle of the signal

A fairly average human voice can produce sounds in the frequency range
100 Hz to 1100 Hz. A sensitive human ear can pick up frequencies from
just over 20 Hz to nearly 20,000 Hz. To provide a telephone system which
will handle this range would be inordinately expensive (but very good
for playing your latest hi-fi record to a distant friend!) Fortunately,
most of the power of the human voice lies within a bandwidth of about
3000 Hz as shown in Figure 3.2. In fact, it has been found that if all
frequencies below a cutoff of 300 Hz and above a cutoff of 3300 Hz are
eliminated, it is still quite possible to recognise the speaker and understand clearly what he is saying (Figure 3.3).

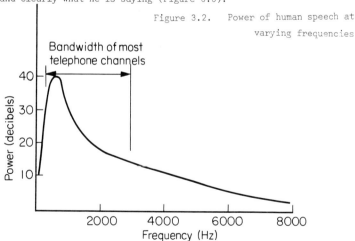

Figure 3.2.   Power of human speech at
varying frequencies

The fact that the voice range between 100 Hz and 300 Hz is lost is the main reason why telephone speech sounds a little 'tinny'. In practice the frequencies outside the range 300 Hz to 3300 Hz are filtered out so that when many telephone conversations are 'packed' into long-distance channels having a very wide bandwidth (each connection having to be 'shifted' to a different passband) there is a decreased danger of 'spillage' between the calls.

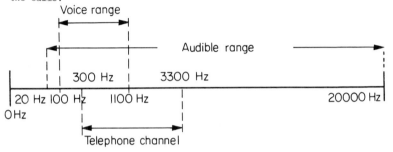

Figure 3.3. Bandwidth of telephone channels

It may be worth noting here that, although most of the world's speech communications facilities operate in this analogue fashion, the British Post Office Corporation is planning a gradual switch-over to a form of digital transmission known as Pulse Code Modulation (PCM). This involves the digitisation of speech so that more calls can be packed into a channel of a given bandwidth, thereby improving the cost/performance ratio of the telephone system as a whole. Such a change will provide benefits for the data transmission user and this is discussed in Chapter 10 on Post Office facilities.

With analogue telephone lines, the bandwidth of such circuits is important because the capacity of a channel to carry information is directly proportional to that bandwidth. In other words, a 300 kHz channel can carry 100 times as many bits per second as a 'standard' 3 kHz channel. In addition to the bandwidth two other factors constrain the speed and accuracy of data transmission on telephone lines. These are *distortion* and *noise*. As mentioned in Chapter 2, distortion is an entirely pre-dictable property of any communications channel whereas noise is of a random nature and is only predictable in a statistical sense.

3.2 DISTORTION

There are three types of distortion we need to consider (the third resulting from a combination of the first two):

12

1.   Phase delay
2.   Attenuation
3.   Jitter or Peak

3.2.1.   Phase Delay

In a perfect communications channel the signal would travel at the
speed of light (186,000 miles/sec). However, in practice, external
influences and the channel itself put up a certain amount of resistance
to the signal such that the speed on a microwave circuit is reduced
to 100,000 miles/sec and on a simple pair of wires 14,000 miles/sec.
The result of this is that there is a finite delay between the transmission of the signal at the source and its reception at the sink. This
time-lag in itself does not present any problems but, unfortunately, the
delay tends to vary according to the frequency of the signal. Generally,
higher frequencies are not delayed as much as lower frequencies as shown
in Figure 3.4. The consequences of this delay (or 'phase shift') become
most clear when considering the situation where two frequencies are being
transmitted over long distances. The lower frequency could be delayed
so much in relation to the higher signal that the two become indistin-
guishable.

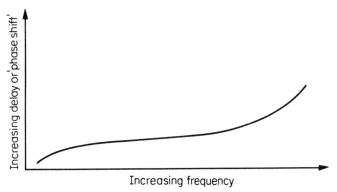

Figure 3.4.   Relationship between frequency and propagation delay

When phase delay distortion becomes critical it is normally dealt
with by the introduction into the circuit of 'delay equalisers'. These
equalisers cause a delay which is complimentary to that of the channel,
the two delays cancelling each other out. The equalisers may be added
to the circuit by the Post Office in order to raise the specification
of the line to a certain standard. Sometimes such components are part of
the modem and this will be discussed later in this Chapter.

13

3.2.2. Attenuation

Attenuation is the loss of power that a signal experiences between the source and the sink. As with phase delay, the loss of power varies according to the frequency of the signal, the higher frequencies being more susceptible as shown by Figure 3.5. Again the solution is to use some kind of equaliser which balances out the effect of attenuation so that all signals are of equal strength.

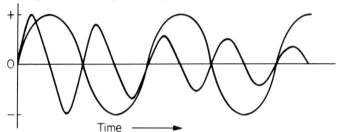

Figure 3.5.   Effect at different frequencies of attenuation distortion

3.2.3. Jitter or Peak

Jitter arises from the combined effect of phase delay and attenuation distortion. Jitter sometimes known as peak distortion, is measured in terms of the variation in the timing of frequency changes of the received signal in relation to the time sequence in which they were transmitted.

3.3 NOISE

Let us now consider the causes and effects of noise. There are four main categories:

1. Thermal noise
2. Impulse noise
3. Induction and Crosstalk
4. Echo

3.3.1. Thermal Noise

Thermal noise is the fundamental of the four. In all substances atoms and molecules are continually in motion and the resultant vibrations and collisions produce a background noise of low but varying strength. If the signal being transmitted becomes too weak, it can be lost in the thermal noise. Analogue signals cannot be completely regenerated as digital (telegraphy) signals can, and must therefore be amplified. However, this amplification of the signal also causes amplification of the noise and does nothing to solve the problem. Thermal noise is also known as 'white noise' or 'Gaussian noise' and can be heard on most channels

14

(e.g. radio) as a hiss when the volume is turned up (and nothing is being transmitted!).

3.3.2. Impulse Noise

Unlike ever-present thermal noise, impulse noise (as its name suggests) is of an intermittant nature. The clicks and short bursts of crackling often heard on a telephone line are typical of impulse noise. Such noise, caused by switching equipment, machinery and even electrical storms, is quite powerful but normally brief in duration as can be seen from Figure 3.6 which contrasts it with thermal noise.

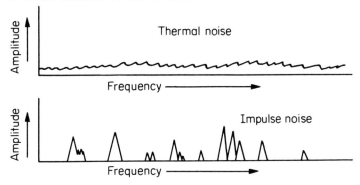

Figure 3.6. Comparison of thermal noise and impulse noise

3.3.3. Induction and Crosstalk

Induction usually occurs on circuits which partially run through multi-line cables (which may contain 50 or more pairs). If any one or more of those circuits is carrying a signal of excessive amplitude it could affect the signals on the other lines. Crosstalk is a form of induction experienced by all telephone users at some time or other and usually originates in multi-circuit cables where the power of one circuit is such that its signal is 'spilling over' to physically adjacent circuits. The extent to which this occurs is dependent upon the proximity of the 'victim' circuit and the distance for which it runs parallel with the 'culprit'.

3.3.4. Echo

Echo on dialled telephone lines is caused by imperfections in the circuit switching equipment which causes the speaker's voice to be transmitted back to him after a slight delay. Echo is only really noticeable on long-distance circuits but can be distracting enough to cause the telecommunications authorities to fit such lines with 'echo suppressors'. These operate in such a way as to break the 'return half' of the circuit

15

while one person is speaking and then to restore that half and break to other half when the second person talks (Figure 3.7).

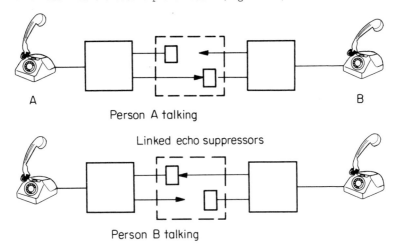

A   B

Person A talking

Linked echo suppressors

Person B talking

Figure 3.7.   Use of echo suppressors

Although it is unlikely that echo itself would be much trouble in a data communications link the suppressors could prove to be embarrassing. In fact, most suppressors can be disabled by placing a signal on the circuit at a particular frequency for a certain duration.

3.4   CIRCUIT TYPES

The physical characteristics of the circuits which telecommunications authorities are normally able to provide and the speeds at which data can be transmitted on them will now be considered. Telephone lines are often referred to as 'circuits' because the line itself is not merely a single wire but a complete electrical connection which requires two wires (Figure 3.8). This circuit normally only exists in the form of a physical pair of wires between the subscriber's telephone equipment and the local tele-phone exchange (with local ends). From there onwards, the circuits are usually carried as sub-channels on co-axial cables, microwave links and so on.

As mentioned previously, these circuits are designed to accommodate the minimum bandwidth essential to the recognisable transmission of the human voice. This imposes constraints on the speed at which data can be accurately transmitted (*see* Chapter 4). In order to increase this band-width, telecommunications authorities provide four-wire circuits comprising two pairs of standard speech lines (Figure 3.9).

16

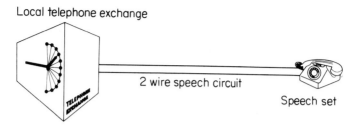

Local telephone exchange

2 wire speech circuit

Speech set

Figure 3.8   Simple telephone circuits

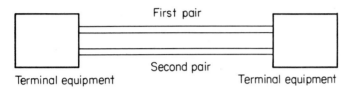

First pair

Second pair

Terminal equipment   Terminal equipment

Figure 3.9.   Four-wire telephone circuit

The only circuit which can be dialled is the standard two-wire speech
line. Furthermore these lines cannot be conditioned in any way because
the actual channels selected by the exchange switching equipment each
time the call is dialled cannot be predicted. However, if a *permanent*
connection between two locations is required, the PTT can allocate specific
local ends and channels by bypassing the switching equipment in intermediate
exchanges. This same technique is used to provide four-wire circuits.
National PTTs will not guarantee a minimum performance for such lines
(in terms of speed, noise and distortion levels) unless they are conditioned. Dialled and dedicated lines linking two locations are described
as *point-to-point*. Dedicated lines can also be supplied in *multipoint* (or
multidrop) configurations where a number of terminal devices share one line
in order to minimise costs (Figure 3.10).

The actual multipoint configurations permissible in each country varies
considerably and reference should be made to the relevant PTT. The British
Post Office rules for multidropping are included in Chapter 10 of this book.
Table 3.1 summarises in general terms, the circuits available (including
telegraph facilities) and the ways in which they can be used.

There is an international standard for conditioned 4-wire leased
circuits known as CCITT M102. The U.K. equivalent is the Tariff T line.

17

(a)

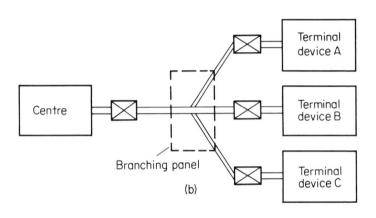

Branching panel

(b)

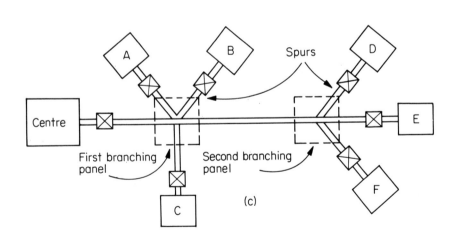

(c)

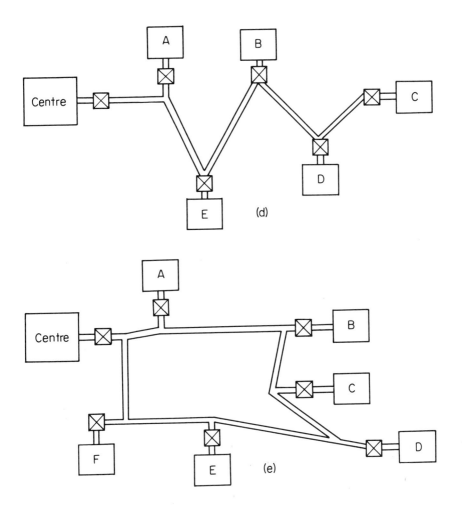

Figure 3.10. Point-to-point and multipoint circuits.

(a) point-to-point circuit (may be dialled)

Note: Two wires are shown as a single line.

(b) Multipoint circuit (must be dedicated).

(c) Common bearers or common service sections.

(d) 'Daisy-chain' type of multidropping. Possible
     only in U.S.A. and some European countries

(e) Loop-type circuit. Possible only in the U.S.A.
     and some European countries

19

Table 3.1 *Types of telecommunications circuits available*

Telegraph	Dialled (Telex)	50 bits/sec
Telegraph	Leased	110 bits/sec
Speech 2-wire	Dialled	600 bits/sec easily. Up to 2400 bits/sec possible.
Speech 2-wire	Conditioned Point-to-point	1200 easily. Up to 9600 with some privately supplied modems.
Speech 4-wire	Unconditioned Point-to-point or multipoint	1200 bits/sec easily. Up to 9600 bits/sec with privately supplied modems.
Speech 4-wire	Conditioned Point-to-point or multipoint	2400 bits/sec easily. Up to 9600 bits/sec (or more) with privately supplied modems.
Wideband (Group of 12 pairs)	Conditioned Point-to-point only	48,000 bits/sec (A limited based service of 240 kbit/sec is available in some countries including the U.K.)

Table 3.2 *Typical Error Rates on Telex and Speech Circuits*

	Transmission rate bits/sec	Bit Error Rate
Telex	50	1 in 50,000
Speech	600	1 in 500,000
	1,200	1 in 200,000
	2,400	1 in 100,000
	4,800	1 in 50,000
	9,600	1 in 5,000

3.5   ERROR RATES

The error rate which might be experienced on an unconditioned tele-communications circuit will vary according to the speed at which it is used.   Table 3.2 gives an indication of the error rates likely to be experienced.

QUESTIONS, DISCUSSION TOPICS AND ASSIGNMENTS

1. Chapter 3 considers only the frequency ranges used by the human voice and ear.   This is the relatively narrow sound band of the whole spectrum of frequencies.   Find out the frequency ranges used by other phenomena, e.g. heat, visible light, infra red light, ultra violet light and radio waves and plot these on a logarithmic scale to show their various relationships.

2. Discuss the difference between *distortion* and *noise*. Describe briefly the main types of distortion and noise.

3. The main advantage of multipoint circuits is that they minimise costs by reducing the number of modems and length of circuit required.   Identify what you would consider to be some of the disadvantages.

4. Table 3.2 indicates the error rate which might be expected on Telex and speech circuits.   Why do the rates increase for higher speeds of transmission?

5. Compare the error rates in Table 3.2 with those which might be expected on the input/output channels of a typical general-purpose computer.

CHAPTER 4
MODEMS AND TRANSMISSION TECHNIQUES

4.1   MODULATION

As has now been established, the major obstacle to the use of the telephone network for data transmission is that it is designed to carry analogue signals whereas computers operate in a discrete (or digital) fashion. This difference obviously dictates that some form of analogue-to-digital (A/D) and digital-to-analogue (D/A) converters are needed at the end of any telephone line which is to be used (Figure 4.1).

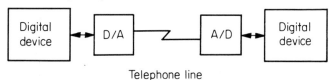

Telephone line

Figure 4.1.   Interface to a telephone line through analogue/digital converters

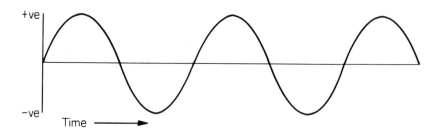

Figure 4.2.   Alternating current signal

The problem is now how to represent data on the telephone line and how this will determine the design of the A/D converters. An easy

22

analogue signal to place on the line is a regular alternating current
which may be represented by the sine wave in Figure 4.2. From Figure
3.1 there are three characteristics of such a waveform which can be used
to describe it. These are:

Frequency (or 'pitch')
Amplitude (or 'loudness')
Phase (or 'timing')

It follows that one of these attributes may be altered in some way to
indicate '0' bits or '1' bits. The modification of the signal is known
as *modulation*. Conversely the detection of such changes and their conversion
to a digital signal is known as *demodulation*.

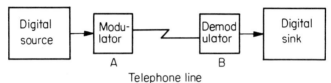

Figure 4.3.   Location of modulator and demodulator in a transmission
               link

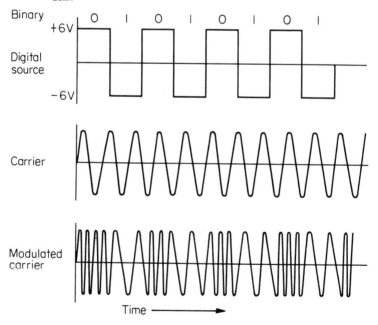

Figure 4.4.   Frequency modulation

23

Consider transmitting a digital signal of '01010101' by modulating
the frequency of the alternating current (ac) on the line (Figure 4.3)
The ac signal (known as the 'carrier') is oscillating at a frequency
of 1300 Hz. It is usual for this signal to be known as the 'mark' or
a '1' bit. To indicate a zero bit we will raise the frequency to 2100 Hz
for a predetermined time interval. It is the rôle of the modulator
('A' in Figure 4.3) to apply the carrier to the line and to raise the
frequency every time the source sends it a '0' bit and to revert to
the carrier frequency when the next '1' bit is received. The demodulator
('B' in Figure 4.3) 'listens' to the line and passes a '1' bit (in digital
form) to the sink for each time interval that it receives the carrier
frequency of 1300 Hz. Each time the frequency goes to 2100 Hz a '0' bit
is passed. (Although there is a time-lag in transmission, it is more
accurate to think of data transmission as being analogous to tapping on
a pipe rather than being like water flowing through the pipe).

Figure 4.4 shows the bit pattern in its original digital form and
as a modulated signal. This very popular form of modulation is often
known as *Frequency Shift Keying (FSK)*.

It is usually essential in data transmission for the sink to be able
to acknowledge receipt of the data sent by the source (otherwise, how are
you to know that it has arrived?) Furthermore, the sink might wish to
assume the rôle of source and transmit data itself; this is the most
common situation where a terminal is 'online' to a computer. For this
reason modulators and demodulators are provided together in the same box
known as a 'modulator-demodulator' (luckily abbreviated to *modem*). Throughout this book the symbol shown in Figure 4.5 will be used to indicate the
position of a modem.

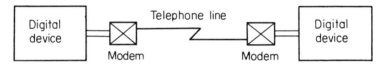

Figure 4.5. Modems

As an alternative to modulating the frequency of the carrier the
amplitude or the phase can be changed as shown in Figure 4.6. It should
be noted that phase modulation usually works slightly differently. A
change in phase indicates a change from '0' to '1' or '1' to '0' depending
upon which the previous bit was. It is not necessary to change the phase
for each bit if we have a sequence of more than one bit of the same kind.

24

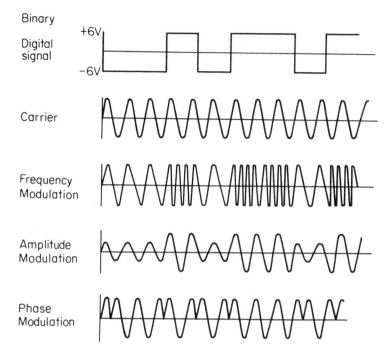

Figure 4.6.   Frequency, amplitude and phase modulation

It is usual at this point in an explanation of data transmission
techniques, to define the term 'baud'. Such definitions are either
so lengthy and complex as to be of value only to those who intend to
delve deep into telecommunications theory, or they are so brief as to
be inaccurate and/or misleading. Basically, the baud rate of a circuit
is the reciprocal of the (average) length of the signal intervals. So
if a carrier is modulated once every 1/300 sec (say) the baud rate is
300. However, it is wrong to think of the baud rate as being synonymous
with 'bits/sec' for the reasons which will become clear in a moment.

4.2   SIGNALLING RATES AND DATA RATES

In Chapter 3, it was shown that the capacity (or 'speed') of a line
was restricted by its bandwidth and the level of noise. The objective
of modem designers has been to achieve speeds as near as possible to a
theoretical maximum. However, the simple approach of using (say) amplitude
modulation and increasingly shortening the signal length merely makes the

link more sensitive to impulse noise and the like. A much more reliable approach has been the use of *multi-level modulation*.

By modulating the frequency, amplitude or phase to *four*-levels it is possible to represent *two* bits of data. For example, the four frequencies shown in Table 4.1 can be used to indicate the range '00' to '11'.

Table 4.1 *Multi-level Frequency Modulation*

Frequency (Hz)	Bit Pattern
1,300	11
1,600	10
1,900	01
2,200	00

Similarly the carrier amplitude can be moved between four levels or the phase might be changed at 0°, 90°, 180° and 270° to represent '11', '10', '01' and '00' respectively. Some modems, for example the CODEX 9600C, use a matrix of phase and amplitude modulation levels to obtain sixteen possible combinations, thus encoding a four bit group (see Table 4.2).

Table 4.2 *Use of a matrix of modulation levels to encode 4 bits*

		Amplitude			
		Level 1	Level 2	Level 3	Level 4
	Change 1	0000	0001	0010	0011
	Change 2	0100	0101	0110	0111
Phase	Change 3	1000	1001	1010	1011
	Change 4	1100	1101	1110	1111

Table 4.3 *Possible Relationships between baud rate and bit rate*

Baud Rate	No. of Modulation Levels	Bit Rate
600	2	600
2,400	2	2,400
2,400	4	4,800
2,400	8	7,200
2,400	4 by 4 matrix	9,600

26

These techniques illustrate the difference between the baud rate and the bit rate of a circuit, i.e. one signal can accommodate more than one bit of data (Table 4.3)

4.3 SYNCHRONISATION

Now that some techniques for modulating the digital signals have been established, the next problem is the timing and synchronisation of the transmission. If some kind of parallel transmission (with one circuit per bit of data) were being used, there would be little trouble in ensuring that bit 1 of the received character was also bit 1 of the transmitted character (Figure 4.7).

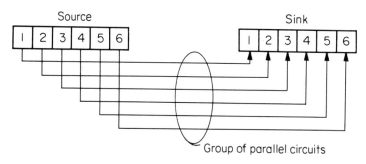

Figure 4.7.   Parallel communications

In using telecommunications facilities to transmit data, it is normal to send bits down the line in a serial fashion. Looking at the problem from the receiving modem, how does it know when to look for a signal and how does it determine which bit is the first of a character? Clearly each transmitting device needs to be fitted with a *clock* (or 'oscillator') to determine the moment at which a signal must be applied to the line. Equally clearly, the receiving device must also have a clock to trigger the 'sampling' of the line for a '0' or '1' bit at the right intervals. The speed of transmission will determine the speed of the clock; 1200 Hz for 1200 baud, 2400 Hz for 2400 baud, etc. Note that if multi-level modulation is being used to transmit data at 4800 bits/sec on a 2400 baud line, the clock speed will still be 2400 Hz.

However, the inclusion of the clocks is not the total solution to the problem: how are the clocks kept in synchronisation? (Figure 4.8). Also, how does the receiver identify the first bit of a character? Two techniques are used to deal with this problem:

    ASYNCHRONOUS (or START-STOP) TRANSMISSION
    SYNCHRONOUS TRANSMISSION

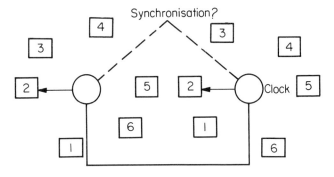

Figure 4.8. Clocking in serial transmission

The first, start-stop, is suitable for low-speed communications (not normally more than 1800 bits/sec), where keyboards and serial printers are directly connected to lines. The second, synchronous transmission, is more suitable for higher speed operation and where large blocks of data are being sent. The reason why the techniques are applicable in these different areas will become evident when the methods of operation are examined in more detail.

4.4   ASYNCHRONOUS TRANSMISSION

Asynchronous transmission is often referred to as 'start-stop' because each character transmitted is preceded by a 'start bit' which 'wakes up' the receiver. The character is followed by at least one stop bit (or sometimes 1·42, 1·5 or 2 bits) to allow both the transmitting and receiving devices to 'get ready' for the next character. Is it possible to manufacture a clock which is 100% accurate? A clock rated at 1200 Hz might in fact operate at 1202 Hz. Also the chance of getting clocks in the transmitting and receiving devices which are exactly the same, is very remote. Given a situation where a device is transmitting at 1199 bits/sec and the receiver begins by sampling the centre of a signal at 1202 Hz the link will probably work successfully for a few characters but eventually the receiver will be unreliably sampling the transition point between bits and then the next bit on as illustrated in Figure 4.9. In spite of this deteriorating effect, slight inaccuracies in the clock can be accommodated so long as the bit stream read is not too long, the signal length is not too short and the clock is restarted for each group of bits (characters) read. The function of the start bit in asynchronous transmission is to start the clock for the duration of a character. The stop bit(s)

28

allow the clocks to be reset and for the communications devices to get
ready for the next character.

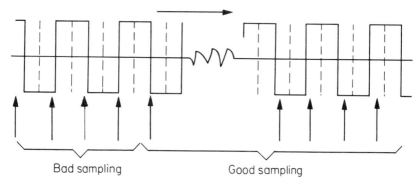

| Indicates the 'centre point' of the signal

↑ Indicates the point at which sampling occurs

Figure 4.9.   Effect of sampling a line with an inaccurate clock

It will be seen from Figure 4.10 that the normal state of the line is
usually mark ('1'). The stop bit will then be mark again. The next
character can then follow immediately (but preceded by another start bit,
of course). Alternatively, there may be varying time intervals between
characters as would be the case if the data were coming from an unbuffered
keyboard. The fact that the line is in an idle condition does not matter
because the clock will not start running until the first start bit arrives.

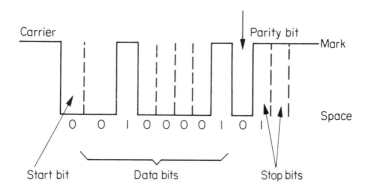

Figure 4.10. Asynchronous character format

29

4.5   SYNCHRONOUS TRANSMISSION

One of the major objections to asynchronous working is that it carries
an overhead of redundant data, 30% in the case of the format in Figure 4.10.
Synchronous communications techniques attempt to overcome this overhead
problem where larger blocks of data are being transmitted. This is done
by having the devices at each end of the line exchange a stream of
'synchronising' bits at periodic intervals. These are sent by the device
which is going to transmit data and the receiving device listens so that
it can get its clock in synchronisation with that of the transmitter.
After the timing bits have been sent real data can be transmitted, but
it must be a continuous stream from a buffer; if the stream stops, it
will be necessary to resynchronise the clocks.

The size of the block which may be transmitted before the clocks need
to be resynchronised varies but is not normally less than about 1000
bits and may be over 10,000 bits. The exact block size may well depend
upon the characteristics of the communicating devices e.g. 80 characters
for card-based data, 132 for a line printer, 1600 for a visual display.
Figure 4.11 shows a typical block of data being transmitted in a synchronous
fashion.

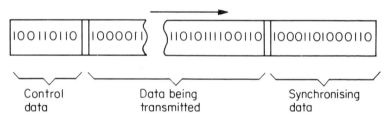

Figure 4.11. Block of data transmitted using synchronous techniques

In order that the timing bits can be distinguished from real data,
they are always sent in a predetermined pattern (*see* Chapter 5). Furthermore, it is essential that 2, 3 or 4 (ideally 4) characters of timing bits
be transmitted, thus minimising the possibilities that (a) random errors
in the line will cause such a sequence to appear or that (b) chance bit
patterns in the data will look like a timing sequence. This ability to
recognise the structure of the timing bits also enables the system to
synchronise with the first data characters.

4.6   EFFICIENCY

Because of this minimum length for the 'synch' bits, the enhanced
efficiency of this type of transmission over start-stop only applies

30

to larger blocks of data (*see* Table 4.4). Some communications devices, in addition to the timing sequence at the beginning of blocks, will also insert automatically synch characters at certain time intervals, e.g. every second, to ensure that the clocks do not go out of phase.

Table 4.4 *Comparative efficiencies of start-stop and synchronous communications techniques*

Number of bits per character	8
Number of start bits	1
Number of stop bits	1
Number of synch characters	4

Number of data characters to be transmitted	Actual number of bits transmitted	
	Start-stop	Synchronous
5	50	72
10	100	112
50	500	432
100	1000	832

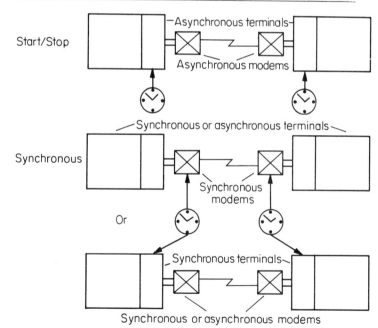

Figure 4.12. Location of clocks in data transmission systems

31

4.7   CLOCKING

We have considered the problems of 'clocking' in the transmission of
data but without mentioning the location of these clocks. Figure 4.12
shows that there are three main arrangements possible. The first is a
completely asynchronous system with 'start-stop' terminals using modems
without clocks. The oscillators are in the modem interfaces and are
activated by the start bit at the beginning of each character. With
synchronous systems there are two possible arrangements. The modem will
be fitted with a clock (thereby making it more expensive and often physically
larger than asynchronous modems) but this will not invariably be used if
the interface in the communications device has its own clock. If the
modem clock is being used, timing 'pulses' are passed to the terminal to
'tell it' when to pass data or sample for data (Figure 4.13). Alternatively,
the modem clock may be inhibited and the clock in the digital device
synchronised to the incoming 'synch' characters. In this case the terminal
itself decides when to transmit or sample data (Figure 4.14). In this
latter configuration it is sometimes possible to use asynchronous modems
in synchronous transmission systems.

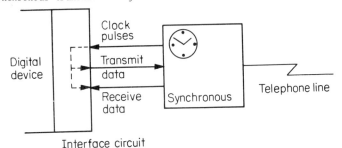

Figure 4.13. Synchronous communications: clocking from the modem

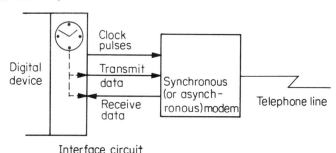

Figure 4.14. Synchronous communications: clocking in the interface
              circuit

32

Acoustic coupler. *By courtesy of GTE Information Systems Ltd.*

An asynchronous modem: Post Office Modem No. 2. *By courtesy of the Post Office Corporation*

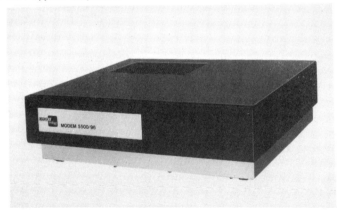

A synchronous modem. The Racal-Milgo Modem 5500/96 is a full-duplex synchronous modem with a data rate of 9600 bits/sec. It can automatically equalise the circuit. *By courtesy of Racal-Milgo Ltd.*

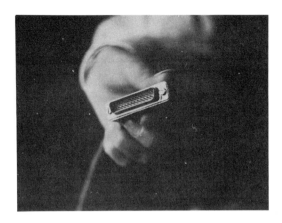

The standard 25 circuit cable and plug arrangement for interfacing
the terminal equipment to the modem. *Photograph by the author*

A telephone set used for establishing calls on the public switched
network. The 'TELE' and 'DATA' buttons can be seen above the dial.
Photograph by the author

4.8   MODEM TYPES

Having established what a modem does, the major categories which are available will now be considered (Figure 4.15). Most modems are directly connected to the telephone line used as shown in Figure 4.16. However, one type of modem has been designed so that it can be used with a standard telephone handset (Figure 4.17). The *acoustical coupler* modulates the digital inputs into speech frequencies which can be transmitted on normal dialled lines, the advantage being that transmission can take place from any location having a telephone. The frequencies adopted are almost always the same as those used in standard low-speed FSK modems (such as the Post Office Modem No. 2). This enables couplers to be used at remote locations but more convenient directly-connected modems to be used at the central site. Some couplers are incorporated in portable terminals. It should be noted that many PTTs do not allow the use of acoustical couplers because of their inability to control the range of signals put on the public telephone network. The Post Office allows (or rather does not try to prevent) the use of these modems and publishes guidelines on their design and use. Most countries still use handsets with carbon granule microphones. Where such handsets are used horizontally instead of vertically the granules tend to pack together causing a loss in signal power. Many synchronous modems now have facilities which introduce to the circuit an 'equalising' signal so that they may be used with some unconditioned lines and make better use of conditioned lines. This 'self equalising' often works in a dynamic fashion so that the modems continually adapt themselves to the condition of the line. Other modems can be manually adapted at regular intervals.

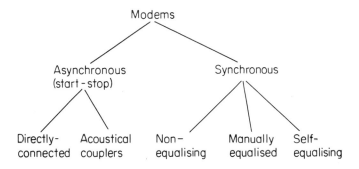

Figure 4.15. Categories of modems

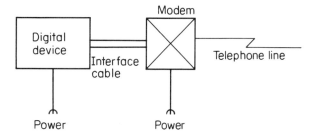

Figure 4.16. Directly connected modem configuration

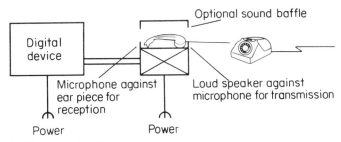

Figure 4.17. Acoustically coupled modem

4.9 INTERFACE

The problem of clocking takes into account the general topic of the interface between the digital device and the modem. There has been developed an interface standard which has gained wide acceptance in the computer industry although some minor variations have occurred. The interface is based upon a 25-connection cable and plug arrangement which can be used for the serial transmission of data to modems in both synchronous and start-stop systems. Internationally this interface conforms to a standard (V.24) produced by the International Consultative Committee for Telephone and Telegraph (CCITT) which is part of the International Telecommunications Union, an agency of the United Nations. In the United States the Electrical Industries Associates have implemented almost identical standards known as EIA RS-232-B and C.

4.10 CCITT STANDARD MODEM INTERFACE

The full CCITT V.24 recommendation is included in Appendix 1 and is summarised in Table 4.5. It will be seen from this that the circuits fall into three main categories; those used for *data*, those used for *control* and those used for *timing*.

36

Table 4.5   *CCITT V.24 Interface Recommendation (100 series only)*

Interchange circuit number	Interchange circuit name	Ground	Data From DCE	Data To DCE	Control From DCE	Control To DCE	Timing From DCE	Timing To DCE
1	2	3	4	5	6	7	8	9
101	Protective ground or earth	X						
102	Signal ground or common return	X						
103	Transmitted data			X				
104	Received data		X					
105	Request to send					X		
106	Ready for sending				X			
107	Data set ready				X			
108/1	Connect data set to line					X		
108/2	Data terminal ready					X		
109	Data channel received line signal detector				X			
110	Signal quality detector				X			
111	Data signalling rate selector (DTE)					X		
112	Data signalling rate selector (DCE)				X			
113	Transmitter signal element timing (DTE)							X
114	Transmitter signal element timing (DCE						X	
115	Receiver signal element timing (DCE)						X	
116	Select standby					X		
117	Standby indicator				X			
118	Transmitted backward channel data			X				
119	Received backward channel data		X					
120	Transmit backward channel line signal					X		
121	Backward channel ready				X			
122	Backward channel received line signal detector				X			
123	Backward channel signal quality detector				X			
124	Select frequency groups					X		
125	Calling indicator				X			
126	Select transmit frequency					X		
127	Select receive frequency					X		
128	Receiver signal element timing (DTE)							X
129	Request to receive					X		
130	Transmit backward tone					X		
131	Received character timing						X	
132	Return to non-data mode					X		
133	Ready for receiving					X		
134	Received data present				X			
191	Transmitted voice answer					X		
192	Received voice answer				X			

There are four data circuits:

Transmitted data $\Big\}$ Main channel
Received data

Transmitted data $\Big\}$ 'Backward' or
Received data 'Supervisory'
Channel

Control circuits, of which there are 26, are described fully in Appendix 1.
An example of their use is a possible sequence to transmit data thus:

Check modem is switched on (107 - Data Set Ready).
If OK, tell modem that the terminal equipment wishes to transmit
(105 - Request to Send).
When OK modem tells terminal to go ahead (106 - Ready for sending).
Terminal starts sending (103 - Transmitted data).

Five circuits are available for timing purposes

Clocking from modem (113) $\Big\}$ Transmission
Clocking from the terminal (114)

Clocking from the modem (115)
Clocking from the terminal (128)
Character timing $\Big\}$ Reception
(from the modem (131))

Strangely enough, the CCITT Recommendation does not include details of
the assignment of circuits to the 25 available pins. There is a separate
standard for this published by the International Standards Organisation
(ISO). Table 4.6 shows pin assignments for a typical start-stop modem
and Table 4.7 for a synchronous modem.

4.11   ALTERNATIVE INTERFACE CONFIGURATIONS

In addition to the interface arrangement shown in Figure 4.16 there
are a number of other possibilities. If the circuit being used is dialled
on the public telephone network it will be necessary for the modem to be
supplied with a telephone (Figure 4.18).

In the U.K. these voice sets have two buttons at the front above the
dial. One is marked 'TELE' and the o.ther 'DATA'. When the TELE button
is depressed a dialling tone will come on the line and the unit can be
used to make ordinary speech calls. If, however, the DATA button is
pressed, control of the line is transferred to the modem. Alternatively,
it is possible for the terminal to be equipped with a switch which will
cause the modem to connect to the line via a circuit in the interface

38

Table 4.6   *Interface Specification for British Post Office*
            Modem No. 1 (Model 5)

Connector pin	CCITT V.24 Designation	Interchange circuit
2	103	Transmitted data
3	104	Received data
4	105	Request to send
5	106	Ready for sending
6	107	Data set ready
7	102	Signal ground
8	109	Data carrier detector
11	111	Data signalling rate
20	108/2	Connect data set to line selector
22	125	Calling indicator

Table 4.7   *Interface Specification for Racal Milgo Modem 4800/72*

Connector pin	CCITT V.24 Designation	Interchange circuit
1	101	Protective ground
2	103	Transmitted data
3	104	Received data
4	105.	Request to send
5	106	Ready for sending
6	107	Data set ready
7	102	Signal ground
8	109	Data carrier detector
9	-	Data modem testing
10	-	Data modem testing
15	114	Transmitted signal element timing
17	115	Receiver signal element timing
21	110	Signal quality detector
23	111	Data signal rate selector

(Figure 4.19). In the U.S.A. and some other countries the speech set
is often integral with the modem. Figure 4.20 illustrates an arrangement
whereby a dialled circuit can be used as an alternative to a dedicated
line, should the latter fail.

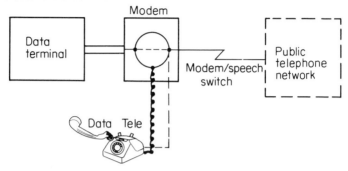

Figure 4.18. Use of the public telephone network (connected to
line from speech set)

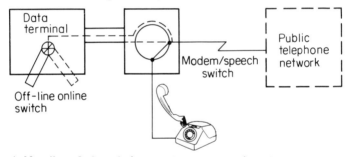

Figure 4.19. Use of the public telephone network (terminal connected
to line)

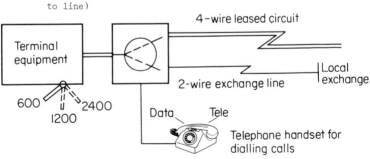

Figure 4.20. Use of PSN as a backup for a leased private line

40

There are a number of techniques available for attaching more than one terminal device to a single modem. The first involves the use of a modem-sharing unit which is plugged into the modem, instead of a single terminal, using the standard interface. In turn, the sharing unit includes a number of standard interface sockets into which the terminals may be connected, perhaps eight (Figure 4.21). The ICL line Sharing Adapter comes in two versions; one model is an unsophisticated device which merely eliminates the need to obtain one modem for each terminal where a number are installed in a single location, thereby giving a 'multipoint' arrangement. The other, more powerful, model enables the computer to 'talk' to the terminals via the adapter as though the whole installation comprised one device, thus minimising the complexity of the central site software.

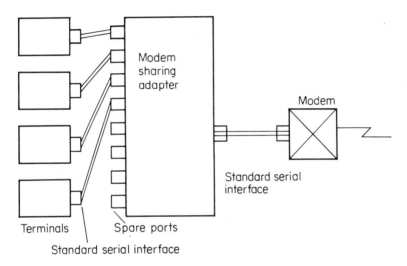

Figure 4.21. Modem sharing adapters

Some manufacturers of terminals incorporate in their communications products (in addition to the usual cable and plug assembly for connection to the modem), a standard interface socket to which may be attached another terminal. Such 'concatenation' may, of course continue if the second terminal also has an interface socket (Figure 4.22). The essential feature of both the above techniques is that they should be *transparent* to the terminals, that is the configuration and method of operation of any attached terminal should be no different from when the terminal is directly connected to the modem.

41

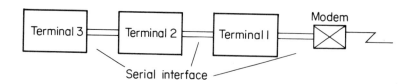

Figure 4.22. Modem sharing by 'concatenating' terminals

4.12   DATA TRANSMISSION ARRANGEMENTS

There are a number of ways in which data can be transmitted;
simplex, half-duplex and full duplex. The generally accepted meanings
of these terms is shown in Figure 4.23. However, the CCITT have recently
produced formal definitions which differ somewhat from the common usage
(which will be adhered to in this book). The CCITT definitions are as
follows:

Simplex: A circuit permitting the transmission of signals
              in either direction, but not both simultaneously
              (commonly called 'half-duplex').

Half-duplex: A full-duplex circuit used by terminal equipment
              which can only operate in a half-duplex fashion.

Full-duplex   Simultaneous transmission in both directions
              (the accepted meaning).

(*see* Chapter 6 for yet another interpretation of these terms).

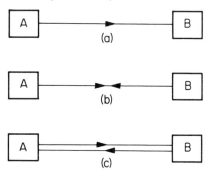

Figure 4.23.   Methods of data transmission
(a)   Simplex: : data in one direction only
(b)   Half-duplex (HDX): data in both directions
      but one way at a time
(c)   Full-duplex or simply duplex (FDX): data in
      both directions at the same time

42

Referring back to the CCITT V.24 serial interface standard in Table 4.5, it will be seen that provision is made for supervisory channels (circuit 118 to 123 etc.,) sometimes called 'return' channels. These channels can be used to indicate such things as success or failure of a transmission without the need to use the data channels. They are not normally used for the transmission of data themselves but can be with suitable modems (Figure 4.24).

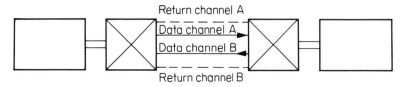

Figure 4.24. Example of the use of supervisory channels

Full-duplex working can be implemented in two ways; by *frequency division multiplexing* (FDM) or by using a physically separate pair for each direction on a 4-wire circuit. FDM usually involves the use of two carriers each with their own 'space' or zero frequencies (Figure 4.25) and is used on British Post Office Modems No. 2. The hard-wired approach is applicable to higher speeds and each modulator is independently connected to the demodulator in the receiving modem (Figure 4.26).

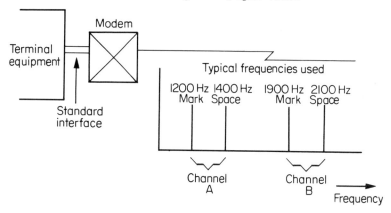

Figure 4.25. A full-duplex circuit using frequency division multiplexing

Some modems (by using FDM and similar techniques) incorporate facilities to 'channel' a circuit in order to provide a number of options. Taking a standard M102 line it might be possible to provide:

43

Two 2400 bits/sec channels (Figure 4.27) or

One 4800 bits/sec channel plus two 2400 bits/sec channels or

One 4800 bits/sec channel plus 8 low-speed teletype channels or

One 2400 bits/sec channel plus one speech circuit (Figure 4.28).

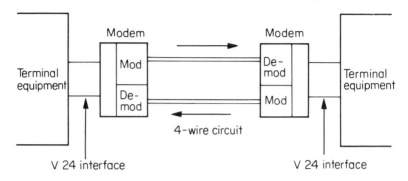

Figure 4.26. A full-duplex circuit using four-wire telephone link

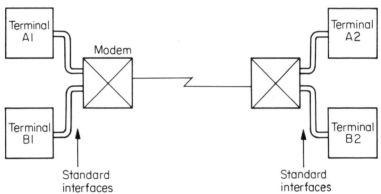

Figure 4.27. Standard four-wire circuit split into two independent

2400 bits/sec full-duplex connections

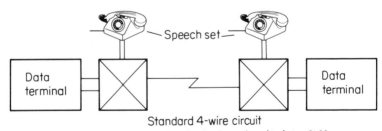

Figure 4.28. Example of modem 'splitting' a circuit into 2400

bits/sec data channel and a simultaneous speech channel

44

The quantity of speech circuits obtained using the above techniques is very poor compared to a full speech-grade line.

QUESTIONS, DISCUSSION TOPICS AND ASSIGNMENTS

1. Figure 4.6 compares, in visual form three different types of modulation. As in Figure 3.1 the waveforms can be represented by a rotating vector. Relate each to a characteristic of the vector, i.e. radius, speed of rotation and direction of rotation.

2. Modems making use of multilevel modulation facilitate transmission at higher rates for a given bandwidth. What might be the disadvantages of such modems?

3. If a stream of bits were being transmitted at a rate of 1200 per second and the receiving (or 'sampling') clock was 3% slower than the transmitting, how many bits would be received accurately before a missampling took place (assuming both clocks started at the same time)?

4. Discuss the need for 'synchronous' transmission techniques. Draw a 'break-even' chart of the effeciencies of synchronous and start-stop transmission for a range of block sizes. List all assumptions made.

5. What, if any, are the advantages of having the clock in the inter-face circuit rather than the modem when using synchronous trans-mission.

6. What are the benefits of acoustic couplers compared with other types of modem? What modification could be made to existing tele-phone speech sets to obviate the need for acoustic couplers?

7. Draw a flowchart of the sequence of events which might take place in the circuitry for handling a synchronous interface such as the one given in Table 4.7. Do this for the transmission and reception of data. Assume that clocking is taking place from the modem.

8. List some of the difficulties involved in the use of the PSTN as backup for leased lines.

9. List some of the advantages and disadvantages of transparent modem-sharing adapters.

10. Consider some of the constraints which might apply to the use of full-duplex transmission.

11. Suggest some possible uses for the arrangement illustrated in Figure 4.28. Why would the speech circuit be unsuitable for use by, say, a production manager to talk to a colleague in another plant?

Opposite

A series of rack-mounted modems being used for international data communications. Such racks are normally used at computer centres in order to reduce the floorspace required and to share power supplies. *By courtesy of Racal-Milgo Ltd.*

A transmission test set. An examination of the controls will reveal the wide variety of tests which may be applied to a circuit. The test set may be plugged into the modem in place of the terminal device and the circuit looped back at the distant modem. The display panel will show counts of the errors detected. *Courtesy Racal-Milgo Ltd.*

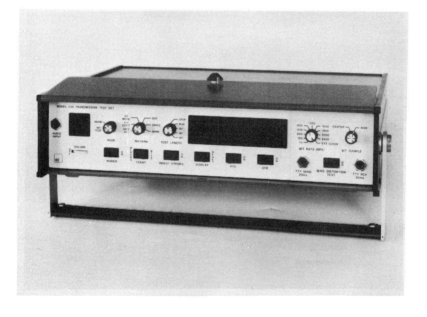

The Burroughs TD.700 visual display terminal works to the same line protocol as that shown in Figure 5.9 and 5.13. *Courtesy of Burroughs Machines Ltd.*

The IBM 3277 visual display is part of the 3270 terminal system the line protocol for which is shown in Figures 5.10 and 5.14. *Courtesy of IBM United Kingdom Ltd.*

CHAPTER 5

LINE CODES AND PROTOCOL

Digital devices, passing between them streams of binary digits over a telecommunications link clearly need to work to some coding convention in order to interpret the data being received. This is done by breaking the bit stream into 'packages' or 'characters' which may be 5, 6, 7 or 8 bits in length. The allocation of a specific meaning to each bit configuration can present considerable problems. Those working the data processing business may well ask 'Why not use the internal computer code?' There are two main reasons why this cannot be done. First of all, telegraph systems existed before computers and could not wait for us to come along and design a code which we would like. Secondly, even the codes used within computers are by no means standardised, which one would we use? This question is not yet resolved, but we are now in the situation of having two standard codes (one 7 bit and one 8 bit) dominating the data communications scene and these will be dealt with later.

5.1   TRANSMISSION CODES

If it were feasible to design a coding system for each teleprocessing application, the choice would be for the minimum size character which would give all the data variety needed. If only the ten numerals 0-9 plus a few 'extras' were wanted, it would be possible to manage with a 4 bit character giving 2^4 or 16 combinations. A 5 bit code provides 2^5 or 32 combinations, enough for an upper case alphabet but no numerals. A 6 bit code is somewhat more useful, having 2^6, 64 characters enough for an upper case alphabet, the numerals and some extras. In order to code upper and lower case alphabets, numerics and still have some 'extras' there is the 7 bit which has 2^7 (128) combinations. The biggest characters currently in use have 8 bits and provide 2^8 (256) bit patterns to play with - more than enough for most applications.

Consider the basic types of data which might be wanted to code. There are four categories:

1. Numeric: 10 digits
2. Alphabetic: 52 including lower case
3. Special Characters: These may include punctuation marks,
                        mathematical symbols and commercial
                        symbols such as £, $, % and @.
4. Control Characters: These characters are used to control
                        either the communications function
                        between the digital devices or the
                        operation of a device at either end
                        of the link.

There are, however, a number of techniques which can be used in order
to expand the scope of the codes with only 5 or 6 bits.

5.2   THE BAUDOT CODE

The main international telegraphy code is the CCITT Alphabet No. 2
popularly referred to as the 'Baudot Code' (after a pioneer of telegraph
techniques who in fact, had nothing to do with this particular convention).
The Baudot Code (Table 5.1) is remarkable for the apparent lack of logic
in the allocation of bit combinations to each character (at least compared
with more recent codes, even those designed by committees!) Its limited
capability is expanded by use of the 'shift' concept. In its normal,
lower case state it has:

The (upper case) alphabet
A blank or 'null' character
Space
and four control characters:
Carriage return
Line feed
Letters shift and
Figures shift

This 'lower case' is known as 'letters shift'. If, while in letters
shift, a 'figures shift' character is received all the same bit patterns
which gave the above meanings are now interpreted to give:

Numerics 0-9
Special characters -, ?, :, (,), .,
   comma, =, /, +.
Control characters WRU? (Who are you?)
   and 'Bell' (To sound an alarm).

50

And three combinations which can be allocated special meanings with each country using the convention. Table 5.1 includes a column showing an American application of the code where these three characters are given the meaning '!' , '&', and '✳'.

Table 5.1 *The 5 bit international telegraph code*
(CCITT International Alphabet No. 2),
Sometimes called the 'Baudot' or more correctly
the 'Murray' code

Start	1	2	3	4	5	Stop	Lower case	Upper case — CCITT standard international telegraph alphabet No.2	Upper case — U.S.A. teletype commercial keyboard
	●	●				●	A	−	−
	●			●	●	●	B	?	?
		●	●	●		●	C	:	:
	●			●		●	D	Who are you?	$
	●					●	E	3	3
	●		●	●		●	F	Note 1	!
		●		●	●	●	G	Note 1	&
			●		●	●	H	Note 1	#
		●	●			●	I	8	8
	●	●		●		●	J	Bell	Bell
	●	●	●	●		●	K	(	(
		●			●	●	L	)	)
			●	●	●	●	M	.	.
			●	●		●	N	,	,
			●		●	●	O	9	9
		●	●		●	●	P	0	0
	●	●	●		●	●	Q	1	1
		●		●		●	R	4	4
	●		●			●	S	,	,
					●	●	T	5	5
	●	●	●			●	U	7	7
		●	●	●	●	●	V	=	;
	●	●			●	●	W	2	2
	●		●	●	●	●	X	/	/
	●		●		●	●	Y	6	6
	●				●	●	Z	+	"
						●	Blank		
	●	●	●	●	●	●	Letters shift	↓	
	●	●		●	●	●	Figures shift	↑	
			●			●	Space	■	
				●		●	Carriage return	<	
		●				●	Line feed	≡	

Note 1: Not allocated internationally; available to each country for internal use.

51

These figures shift interpretations apply until a 'letters shift' control
character is reached. The control characters available in letters shift
do not, for obvious reasons change in figure shift.

Clearly, the Baudot code is far from suitable for use in computers;
it was just not designed for the job. So, initially, the use of standard
telegraph devices such as the Teletype in the U.S.A. and the Teleprinters
in the U.K. (see Chapter 6) for communications with computers presented
the problem of code incompatibility. It was (and often still is) necessary for the computer to translate its incoming messages from the line
code to its internal code and vice versa for data being transmitted to
terminals.

5.3 BINARY CODED DECIMAL

During the reign of its second generation of computers, the 1400
series, IBM introduced a number of data communications terminals designed
for business use. These were engineered to work with a 7 bit code which
was much more compatible with the code used in the computer. In actual
fact, the convention was based upon a 6 bit code but instead of using
'shift' control characters to extend its range, a 'shift bit' was added
to each character making it a 7 bit code in all (Table 5.2).

In this instance the code does have a logical structure e.g. decimal
1 to 9, is represented by binary '1' to '1001'. The normal shift contains:

Numeric 0-9

Alphabetics (lower case)

Special characters ., $, comma, /, ' (quote), &, -, @.

In the upper shift (i.e. S-bit = '1') we have:-

Alphabetics (upper case)

Special characters =, c (cents), ;, :, ^{o}C, ' (quote), -, +, (,), .,
! comma, ?, ±, *.

As with the Baudot code the control characters are the same in either
shift. This code is still widely used in some areas and the extensive
terminal networks of Lloyds Bank,The Halifax Building Society and the
National & Commercial Banking Group all use a version of BCD known as
'1050' code (or 'Paper Tape and Transmission Code'(PTTC)), after the
IBM terminal it was first conceived for. It must be pointed out that
BCD is not a standard but a *technique* and other manufacturers (e.g.
Univac) have a 'BCD' code which is quite different from the one in
Table 5.2.

Table 5.2   IBM *Binary Coded Decimal* (BCD)

Normal shift   DATA CHARACTERS: Upper shift

Character	S	B	A	8	4	2	1	Parity
1	0	0	0	0	0	0	1	0
2	0	0	0	0	0	1	0	0
3	0	0	0	0	0	1	1	1
4	0	0	0	0	1	0	0	0
5	0	0	0	0	1	0	1	1
6	0	0	0	0	1	1	0	1
7	0	0	0	0	1	1	1	0
8	0	0	0	1	0	0	0	0
9	0	0	0	1	0	0	1	1
0	0	0	0	1	0	1	0	1
a	–	1	1	0	0	0	1	0
b	0	1	1	0	0	1	0	0
c	0	1	1	0	0	1	1	1
d	0	1	1	0	1	0	0	0
e	0	1	1	0	1	0	1	1
f	0	1	1	0	1	1	0	1
g	0	1	1	0	1	1	1	0
h	0	1	1	1	0	0	0	0
i	0	1	1	1	0	0	1	1
j	0	1	0	0	0	0	1	1
. k	0	1	0	0	0	1	0	1
l	0	1	0	0	0	1	1	0
m	0	1	0	0	1	0	0	1
n	0	1	0	0	1	0	1	0
o	0	1	0	0	1	1	0	0
p	0	1	0	0	1	1	1	1
q	0	1	0	1	0	0	0	1
r	0	1	0	1	0	0	1	0
s	0	0	1	0	0	1	0	1
t	0	0	1	0	0	1	1	0
u	0	0	1	0	1	0	0	1
v	0	0	1	0	1	0	1	0
w	0	0	1	0	1	1	0	0
x	0	0	1	0	1	1	1	1
y	0	0	1	1	0	0	0	1
z	0	0	1	1	0	0	1	0
	0	1	1	1	0	1	1	0
$	0	1	0	1	0	1	1	0
.	0	0	1	1	0	1	1	1
/	0	0	1	0	0	0	1	1
'	0	0	0	1	0	1	1	0
&	0	1	1	0	0	0	0	1
–	0	1	0	0	0	0	0	0
@	0	0	1	0	0	0	0	0

Character	S	B	A	8	4	2	1	Parity
=	1	0	0	0	0	0	1	
c	1	0	0	0	0	1	0	1
,	1	0	0	0	0	1	1	1
.	1	0	0	0	1	0	0	0
*C	1	0	0	0	1	0	1	1
.	1	0	0	0	1	1	0	0
–	1	0	0	0	1	1	1	0
+	1	0	0	1	0	0	0	1
(	1	0	0	1	0	0	1	0
)	1	0	0	1	0	1	0	0
A	1	1	1	0	0	0	1	1
B	1	1	1	0	0	1	0	1
C	1	1	1	0	0	1	1	0
D	1	1	1	0	1	0	0	1
E	1	1	1	0	1	0	1	0
F	1	1	1	0	1	1	0	0
G	1	1	1	0	1	1	1	1
H	1	1	1	1	0	0	0	1
I	1	1	1	1	0	0	1	0
J	1	1	0	0	0	0	1	0
K	1	1	0	0	0	1	0	0
L	1	1	0	0	0	1	1	1
M	1	1	0	0	1	0	0	0
N	1	1	0	0	1	0	1	1
O	1	1	0	0	1	1	0	1
P	1	1	0	0	1	1	1	0
Q	1	1	0	1	0	0	0	0
R	1	1	0	1	0	0	1	1
S	1	0	1	0	0	1	0	0
T	1	0	1	0	0	1	1	1
U	1	0	1	0	1	0	0	0
V	1	0	1	0	1	0	1	1
W	1	0	1	0	1	1	0	1
X	1	0	1	0	1	1	1	0
Y	1	0	1	1	0	0	0	0
Z	1	0	1	1	0	0	1	1
.	1	1	1	1	0	1	1	1
'	1	1	0	1	0	1	1	0
,	1	0	1	1	0	1	1	0
?	1	0	1	0	0	0	1	1
±	1	0	0	1	0	1	1	0
+	1	1	1	0	0	0	0	0
–	1	1	0	0	0	0	0	0
*	1	0	1	0	0	0	0	1

CONTROL CHARACTERS   (Either shift – s ignored)

Backspace		1	0	1	1	1	0
End of transfer		0	0	1	1	1	1
Delete		1	1	1	1	1	1
Down-shift		1	1	1	1	1	0
Carriage return		1	0	1	1	0	1
Prefix		0	1	1	1	1	1
Idle		1	0	1	1	1	1
Reader stop		0	0	1	1	0	1
Space		0	0	0	0	0	0
End of block		0	1	1	1	1	0
Up-shift		0	0	1	1	1	0
Line feed		0	1	1	1	0	1
Tab		1	1	1	1	0	1
Restore		1	0	1	1	0	0
Bypass		0	1	1	1	0	0
End of heading		0	0	1	0	1	1
Punch on		0	0	1	1	0	0
Punch off		1	1	1	1	0	0

5.4   THE ASCII CODE

In a somewhat successful attempt to forstall an impending prolifer-
ation of codes, the American Standards Association (now known as ANSI,
The American National Standards Institute) produced a 7 bit code gener
called ASCII-7; the American Standard Code for Information Interchang
(Table 5.3). In addition to meeting the minimum requirement of numera
and an upper and lower case alphabet, ASCII provided a comprehensive s
of special characters and no less than 32 pre-assigned control charac·

The disadvantage of IBM's BCD codes was that they are based on a computer code which itself was based on the coding used on 80 column Hollerith card.

With ASCII it was possible to start from 'square one' and use all possible 128 combinations to best effect. The control characters are contained within columns 0 and 1 (Table 5.3) and have the following meanings.

Table 5.3   *American Standards Association 7 bit Standard Code for Information Interchange (ASCII)*

USASCII X3.4.1967

b_4 b_3 b_2 b_1	Column / Row	0	1	2	3	4	5	6	7
0 0 0 0	0	NUL	DLE	SP	0	@	P	`	p
0 0 0 1	1	SOH	DC1	!	1	A	Q	a	q
0 0 1 0	2	STX	DC2	"	2	B	R	b	r
0 0 1 1	3	ETX	DC3	#	3	C	S	c	s
0 1 0 0	4	EOT	DC4	$	4	D	T	d	t
0 1 0 1	5	ENQ	NAK	%	5	E	U	e	u
0 1 1 0	6	ACK	SYN	&	6	F	V	f	v
0 1 1 1	7	BEL	ETB	'	7	G	W	g	w
1 0 0 0	8	BS	CAN	(	8	H	X	h	x
1 0 0 1	9	HT	EM	)	9	I	Y	i	y
1 0 1 0	10	LF	SUB	*	:	J	Z	j	z
1 0 1 1	11	VT	ESC	+	;	K	[	k	{
1 1 0 0	12	FF	FS	,		L	\	l	'
1 1 0 1	13	CR	GS	-	=	M	]	m	}
1 1 1 0	14	SO	RS	.	>	N	∧	n	~
1 1 1 1	15	SI	US	/	?	O	_	o	DEL

Bit 7 = Most Significant Bit

COLUMN 0

NUL (Null):	All-zero 'blank' character which may be used as a filler. This is not the same as SP (Space).
SOH (Start of Heating):	Used to indicate the start of control information at the beginning of a block of data.
STX (Start of Text):	Indicates the end of the heading and the beginning of the actual text of the message.
EXT (End of Text):	Used to indicate the end of message text which started with an STX.
EOT (End of Transmission):	Signifies the end of a transmission containing one or more texts. EOT is sometimes used to 'clear' or 'reset' a line.
ENQ (Enquiry):	Request for response. May be sent to or received from a terminal. Often occurs at the end of a polling sequence.
ACK (Acknowledge):	Positive acknowledgement which is commonly used to confirm the receipt of a 'good' i.e. accurate, message or to respond favourably to a poll.
BEL (Bell):	Character used to activate a visible, audible (or tactile?) alarm at the receiving terminal device.
BS (Backspace):	Used to request the backward (i.e. leftward) movement of the receiving device's printing mechanism or, if the receiver is a visual display, the cursor.
HT (Horizontal Tab):	This character initiates the rightward movement of the print mechanism (or VDU cursor) to the text tab stop (or variable field) set on the receiving device.
LF (Line Feed):	Causes the print mechanism (or cursor) of the receiving device to effectively relocate itself to the same position (relative to the margins) on the next line of the stationery (or screen).
VT (Vertical Tab):	Causes the stationery control mechanism to feed the paper to the next preassigned line, e.g. the column totals line. Not normally used on visual displays.

FF (Form Feed):   Used to cause the stationery control mechanism to move the paper so that the print mechanism is positioned at the start of the next page or form. Not often used on visual display.

CR (Carriage Return):   Move the print mechanism (or cursor) to the first position on the same line. N.B. The ASCII convention does not allow for 'CRLF' (Carriage Return/Line Feed) i.e. one character to cause the print mechanism or cursor to move to the first position of the *next* line unless the device manufacturer assigns one of the 'DC' characters to this function.

SO (Shift Out):   Used to indicate that all successive characters may be interpreted outside the normally assigned meanings until an SI (Shift In) character is received.

SI (Shift In):   Indicate the end of an SO (Shift Out) phase and that all successive characters will be attributed their standard meanings.

COLUMN 1

DLE (Data Link Escape):   This character is used to change the meaning of at least one following character. This enables extra control characters to be assigned and for any coding convention to be used for data characters. (See text for more detailed narrative on the use of DLE.)

DC1 ⎫
DC2 ⎬   (Device Control): Reserved for the control of terminal 'peripherals' and/or special features, the exact meanings to be assigned by the device manufacturer.
DC3 ⎬
DC4 ⎭

NAK (Negative Acknowledgement):   Used as a negative response sent by a receiving device. May indicate, for example, bad parity in received message or inability to respond to a poll with data.

SYN (Synchronous Idle):   Used to identify a sequence of synchronising bits. These may occur preceding data, embedded in data, or being sent continuously as 'idle' characters when no data is being

	transmitted.
ETB (End of Transmission Block):	Used to indicate the end of a 'physical' block of data where this may not coincide with the 'logical' format of the data being transmitted.
CAN (Cancel):	Used to signify that all preceding data in the block or message should be ignored. This character often corresponds to a key or a serial terminal device which the operator can use when he or she notices an error in a message just typed. The computer may respond with an invitation to re-enter the data.
EM (End of Medium):	Indicates the physical (rather than logical) end of data from some medium, e.g. cards, paper tape, cassette tape, etc.
SUB (Substitute):	Normally used to replace an invalid character (perhaps having bad parity). As this character is not printable (or displayable) terminal designers often arrange for it to show as a special symbol e.g. '⸮' reverse question mark or '■' blob!
ESC (Escape):	Another character which the designers of the communications system can use to extend the standard code. It normally means 'the next n character to have a special meaning'.

FS (File Separator): ⎫	Information delimiters to be used as required
GS (GROUP Separator): ⎬	by the equipment supplier and/or system designer.
RS (Record Separator):⎬	However, units are subsets of records which are
US (Unit Separator): ⎭	subsets of groups which are subsets of files.

Other characters

All other characters are displayable except DEL (Delete) which has a value of all binary ones: 1111.111. This is normally used in physical media to delete characters by 'overwriting' them e.g. punching a hole in every channel on a paper tape.

Although the 128 possible combinations of the 7 bit might initially seem to be more than enough, the only 'spares' allowed by the now widely accepted ASCII convention are the four 'Device Control' characters.

However, use of *escape characters* introduces a fair degree of flexibility and three types are available. Even though the standard alphabet is available in upper and lower case, the use of the SO (Shift Out) and SI (Shift In) codes could be used, perhaps to indicate that an italic print style is required on a special device. ESC (Escape) and DLE (Data Link Escape) are essentially similar in that they are used to assign alternative meanings to a contiguous set of following characters. Consider, for example, a terminal has been attached to a fairly sophisticated ancilliary device (maybe a cassette tape unit) operating under the control, of say, eight possible pairs of control characters. Its use might be implemented by including circuitry which looks out for ESC and then takes the next two characters (which could be coded as letters of the alphabet) and interprets from them the required control functions.

Data Link Escape (DLE) is often used to facilitate a technique known as *transparent text mode*. This is required when it is necessary to transmit data containing unpredictable bit patterns, which, if interpreted according to the ASCII convention, could give rise to spurious control characters thereby making orderly communications impossible. An example of such data would be a program in object-code. In its simplest form transparent text mode merely involves the insertion of DLE in front of every *real* control character.

5.5   EBCDIC

Currently the major 8 bit code in use is IBM's Extended Binary Coded Decimal Interchange Code (EBCDIC) which is used in their 360/370 range of computers as well as compatible devices such as the ICL System 4 and the Univac 9000 series. Although the extra bit provides more 'spare' combinations (as well as more expense in the cost of the circuits to handle them), EBCDIC has fewer designated control characters than 7 bit ASCII, in fact, 16 rather than 32 (*see* Table 5.4). However, IBM markets a range of terminals which conforms to a standard protocol known as *Binary Synchronous* (Chapter 6). BSC or 'Bisync' is based upon the EBCDIC code but can also transmit ASCII characters.

The standard set of EBCDIC control characters has, therefore, been extended to provide the addition control required by BSC devices (Table 5.9). Some of these additions always comprise *two* characters. BSC control characters carry basically the same designations as ASCII's i.e. STX, ETX, ACK, NAK, etc., and their use will be described later in this chapter when we talk about line protocols generally.

Table 5.4   *Extended Binary Coded Decimal Interchange Code*

Bit positions 1,2,3,4

HEX		0	1	2	3	4	5	6	7	8	9	A	B	C	D	E	F
		0000	0001	0010	0011	0100	0101	0110	0111	1000	1001	1010	1011	1100	1101	1110	1111
0	0000	NUL				Blank	B	–						>	<	t	0
1	0001						/			a	j			A	J		1
2	0010									b	k	s		B	K	S	2
3	0011									c	l	t		C	L	T	3
4	0100	PF	RES	BYP	PN					d	m	u		D	M	U	4
5	0101	HT	NL	LF	RS					e	n	v		E	N	V	5
6	0110	LC	BS	EOB	UC					f	o	w		F	O	W	6
7	0111	DEL	IDL	PRE	EOT					g	p	x		G	P	X	7
8	1000									h	q	y		H	Q	Y	8
9	1001						/		"	i	r	z		I	R	Z	9
A	1010					?	!		:								
B	1011					.	S	,	#								
C	1100					←	•	%	@								
D	1101					(	)	ˇ	'								
E	1110					+	;	–	=								
F	1111					•	¢	±	/								

Bit positions 5,6,7,8

Bit I = Most significant bit

5.6   INTERNATIONAL ALPHABET NO. 5

In 1968, the CCITT published 'IA5' (Table 5.5) which gives international recognition to ASCII-7 which was released the previous year.
Control characters have been split into four main groups:

TC   Transmission Control

FE   Format Effector

DC   Device Control

IS   Information Separator

The accepted meanings of the control characters is essentially the same
but CCITT and ISO (International Standards Organisation) may produce
yet more recommendations on aspects, e.g. use of TC and escape characters.

At the same time that IA5 was published (as Recommendation V3) the
CCITT also published a report on its use (Recommendation V4). They
covered such factors as:

the positioning of the parity bit

use of even parity for paper tape and odd for
  transmission

transmission sequence (least significant bit first)

number of start and stop bits

For further information it is recommended that the relevant Recommendations
be obtained.

Table 5.5   CCITT International Alphabet No. 5   (Recommendation V3 1968)

			b7	0	0	0	0	1	1	1	1
			b6	0	0	1	1	0	0	1	1
			b5	0	1	0	1	0	1	0	1
b4	b3	b2	b1 \ Column / Row	0	1	2	3	4	5	6	7
0	0	0	0	NUL	(TC₇)DLE	SP	0	(@)	P	`	p
0	0	0	1	(TC₁)SOH	DC₁	!	1	A	Q	a	q
0	0	1	2	(TC₂)STX	DC₂	"	2	B	R	b	r
0	0	1	3	(TC₃)ETX	DC₃	£	3	C	S	c	s
0	1	0	4	(TC₄)EOT	DC₄	$	4	D	T	d	t
0	1	0	5	(TC₅)ENQ	(TC₈)NAK	%	5	E	U	e	u
0	1	1	6	(TC₆)ACK	(TC₉)SYN	&	6	F	V	f	v
0	1	1	7	BEL	(TC₁₀)ETB	'	7	G	W	g	w
1	0	0	8	FE₀(BS)	CAN	(	8	H	X	h	x
1	0	0	9	FE₁(HT)	EM	)	9	I	Y	i	y
1	0	1	10	FE₂(LF)	SUB	*	:	J	Z	j	z
1	0	1	11	FE₃(VT)	ESC	+	;	K	([)	k	
1	1	0	12	FE₄(FF)	IS₄(FS)	,	<	L	(])	l	
1	1	0	13	FE₅(CR)	IS₃(GS)	-	=	M	(])	m	
1	1	1	14	SO	IS₂(RS)	.	>	N	^	n	
1	1	1	15	SI	IS₁(US)	/	?	O	_	o	DEL

bits b7 b6 b5 b4 b3 b2 b1

5.7   ERROR CONTROL

The well-worn adage 'garbage in - garbage out' is still as true as it ever was. All that has changed is that error handling techniques have become increasingly sophisticated over the past ten years - especially within the computer itself. Indeed press headlines about 'computer errors' (as opposed to programming errors) are now so far removed from reality as to be absurd. Certainly hardware failures do occur in computers, but the likelihood of any resulting corrupted data remaining undetected is slight indeed. However, data stored within modern computers is generally held on magnetic media manufactured to narrow tolerances, read or recorded by sophisticated control units and data transmission between components is along carefully screened multi-core cables.

The development towards terminal-based systems presents new problems in the area of error control. Many such systems are now so extensive that all data entering the computer arrives via telephone lines; lines on which error-causing noise is an unavoidable phenomenon. Communication systems must be designed on the assumption that unpredictable errors of varying magnitude will inevitably occur. Furthermore, a compromise needs to be sought between the degree of redundancy inherent in all error control systems and the speed of the circuits available; all relatively slower than those attainable within a computer system. Two factors need to be considered:

Error detection

Error correction

(It is not within the scope of this book, to discuss operator originated errors which is more within the realm of systems design in general and ergonomics in particular).

Error detection and correction generally occurs at two levels:

1.   Character checking
2.   Block checking

5.7.1.   Character Checking

The most widely used method of error checking within characters is that used within most computers:

Odd parity or Even parity

This technique involves the addition of one bit to the character (whatever its size) and the value of the 'check bit' or 'parity' bit is such as to make the total number of one-bits in the character odd or even (Table 5.6)

Table 5.6   *Examples of odd and even parity*

	Data Bits							Check Bits	
Odd Parity	0	1	1	0	1	0	0	0	Good
	1	0	1	1	0	1	0	1	
	1	1	0	1	1	0	1	1	Bad
	0	1	1	0	0	0	0	0	
Even Parity	0	0	1	0	1	0	1	1	Good
	1	1	1	1	1	1	1	1	
	1	1	1	1	1	1	0	1	Bad
	0	1	0	0	1	1	0	0	

Such an arrangement is easy to implement on communications systems; the transmitting equipment (*not* the modem) automatically attaches a check bit which is the modulo-2 sum (or its complement) of the bits in the character. The receiving device does the same and compares the calculated check bit with that transmitted. If interference on the line has caused a bit to be misread ('1' as '0' or '0' as '1') the check will fail and the data will need to be retransmitted. However, if *two* bits within the same character are reversed the error will remain undetected.

Table 5.7   *Two-out-of-five code*

Binary value	Decimal
00110	0
00011	1
00101	2
01001	3
01010	4
01100	5
10001	6
10010	7
10100	8
11000	9

An alternative method of checking characters is the use of *fixed weight* codes, sometimes called *M out of N codes*. These are based upon the design of the coding convention in such a way that a fixed number of bits within the characters are always binary ones. Examples of such codes are:

Two-out-of-five

Four-out-of-eight

Biquinary

The first 2-out-of-5 is a little used code for numerics (Table 5.7)
The 4-out-of-8 code was developed by IBM for use on various second-
generation synchronous devices. Biquinary (2-out-of-7) was the code
used on the almost antique IBM 650 computer but not for transmission
purposes (Table 5.8). Although fixed weight codes are safer than parity
checks, the level of redundancy is very high and, for the purposes of
modern communications systems, generally unacceptable.

Table 5.8   *Biquinary code (2-out-of-7)*

Binary value		Decimal
00001	01	0
00010	01	1
00100	01	2
01000	01	3
10000	01	4
00001	10	5
00010	10	6
00100	10	7
01000	10	8
10000	10	9

The *hamming distance* is the difference between the values of adjacent
characters within any code. This is usually 1. The effect of using a
parity bit is to increase the hamming distance to 2. Fixed weight codes
increase the hamming distance whilst providing a very simple way of checking
the validity of the character. More sophisticated techniques have been
developed which not only detect an error in a character, but can correct
it as well. An example of this is the *hamming code*. A hamming code
for a 4 bit character is shown in Figure 5.1. Check bit 1 provides even
parity for databits 3, 5 and 7; check bit 2 for databits 3, 6 and 7; and
check bit 4 for databits 5, 6 and 7. Thus each information bit is covered
by two check bits (three in the case of bit 7).

A failure of only one combination will indicate that the check bit is
wrong. Two or more failures will indicate that a databit has been corrupted (Table 5.9)

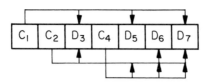

Figure 5.1.   The four-bit Hamming code. C's are the checkbits,
              D's are the data bits.

Table 5.9   *Error location using the Hamming Code*

Check bits (A '1' indicates parity error - not value of bit) C_4 C_2 C_1			Bit in Error
0	0	0	None
0	0	1	C_1
0	1	0	C_2
0	1	1	D_3
1	0	0	C_4
1	0	1	D_5
1	1	0	D_6
1	1	1	D_7

Objections to the Hamming Code are two-fold. Firstly, the level of
redundancy is high; a 7 bit code would require 4 check bits, making
11 bits in all. Secondly, the cost of the circuitry to handle 11 bit
characters and the more complex checking algorithm would be relatively
high.

5.7.2.   Block Checking

   By far the most popular form of block checking is the application of
horizontal parity (longitudinal redundancy check). This involves the
addition of an extra character to the end of the block (Figure 5.2).
This technique can be used on blocks of any length although some systems
transmit fixed-length blocks. The advantage of having the matrix arrangement is that single bit errors can be detected and corrected 'in flight'
(Figure 5.3 (a)). However, two or more errors in the same block cannot
be corrected and a retransmission will be necessary (Figure 5.3 (b)).

64

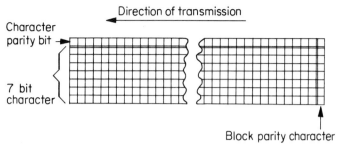

Figure 5.2. Use of block parity checking. Each bit in the block
parity character provides odd or even parity for a
row of equivalent bit positions

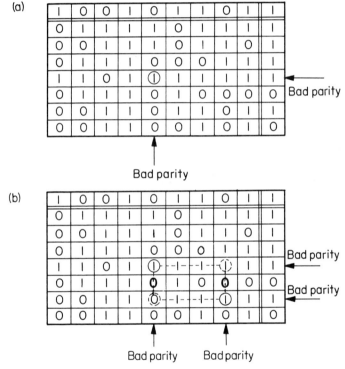

Figure 5.3. Vertical and horizontal parity checking. The bits
in error are indicated by a heavy circle. (a) One bit
error. (b) Two bit errors. There is no way of telling
whether the positions marked with a broken circle are the
ones causing the parity failure

65

The cyclical redundancy check (Figure 5.4) is a method of parity checking that can be used at a character level but is more commonly used for whole blocks with, perhaps, no verification of individual characters. The system involves the generation of one or two check characters, each bit giving odd or even parity to a different pattern of bits (regardless of character boundaries) throughout the block.

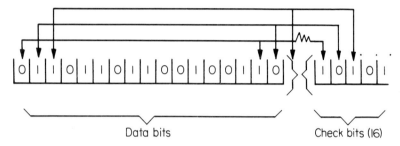

Figure 5.4. Cyclical redundancy check

5.8 LINE PROTOCOL

Code conventions provide only the 'vocabulary' of the communications dialogue between terminal and computer. No one has yet succeeded in establishing a standard 'syntax' or line control procedure. Two main classes of protocol have been developed:

Contention (including Conversational)

Polling

The contention approach is used only on point-to-point lines. Polling is used on multipoint circuits, including those having only one terminal attached. A fundamental feature of all the techniques described is that it is *never* assumed that a block of data has arrived safely unless a positive acknowledgement is received by the transmitting device. (For reasons of simplicity the figures in this chapter showing line protocol do not allow for full duplex working.)

5.9 CONTENTION

Contention or 'point-to-point' line control operates in such a way that no one end of the link has permanent control over the dialogue. Figure 5.5 illustrates a typical sequence.

(a) When an end station wishes to transmit it sends an ENQ character and waits.

(b) If the other end can receive the data it will respond with an ACK character.

(c) The first end station (the computer in our example) then transmits the data.

(d) If the parity and any other checks are all successful then the receiver will reply with ACK. Otherwise it will send NAK and wait for a retransmission.

(e) The transmitter then sends EOT to terminate the dialogue.

If the terminal had wished to send a message, the sequence would have been exactly the same but with the roles of transmitter and receiver reversed.

5.10   TIMEOUTS

The problem of what happens if both ends sent ENQ at the same instant is settled by the concept of the *timeout*. Because of the varying speeds with which individual devices in a data communications system will respond, it is not possible to design the hardware (and software) components to work to exact time intervals. However, it is neither practical nor safe to leave all timing factors open ended and limits must be set. This is done by incorporating clocks which are preset to limits dictated by the delay they will measure. There are two main timeouts:

Response timeout

Text timeout

The former is used where a reply to a control character is required from a device at the other end of a line. It is usually set between 1-5 sec. Under normal circumstances the response to the ENQ in Figure 5.5 (for example) should be measured in milliseconds. However, if the terminal is not switched on, or the line has failed there would be no reply at all. But the computer cannot wait forever and the timeout 'alarm clock' which was set by the transmission of the ENQ will 'ring' and the program can intervene to print a message on the console typewriter or on the network controller's terminal.

The 'text' timeout is used when a string of two or more characters is being transmitted (primarily in asynchronous communications). After each character is received the clock is reset to zero. If the delay between one character and the next is so long that the clock value is exceeded then the program will be interrupted so that special action can be taken. The text timeout is particularly applicable where unbuffered keyboards are being used and prevents the situation where an operator might

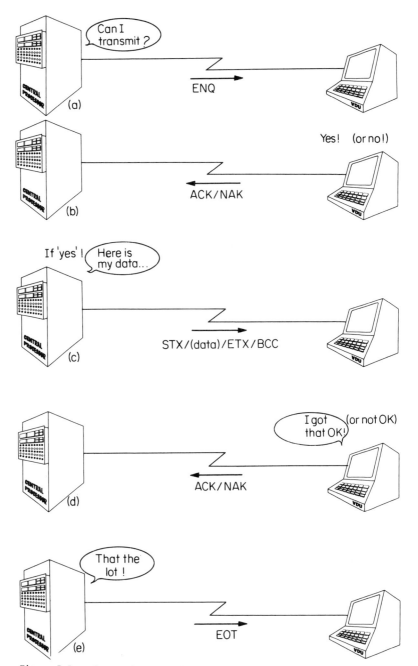

Figure 5.5.   Contention or point-to-point line protocol

go off for a coffee in the middle of a message and leave the line and some of the CPU capacity needlessly tied up. How then, can the timeout concept be applied to the contention problem when both ends want to transmit at the same time? The answer is that the engineer sets the timeout clocks to different values, let us say 3 sec at the terminal end and 5 sec at the computer end (Figure 5.6). Because each device transmitted ENQ it will not have been listening for ENQ from the other end and will not, therefore, send ACK or NAK. Accordingly everything will go quiet until the respective timeout 'alarms' go off and the devices send ENQ again. But the terminal (or whatever) only waited for 3 sec and 'got in' before the computer.

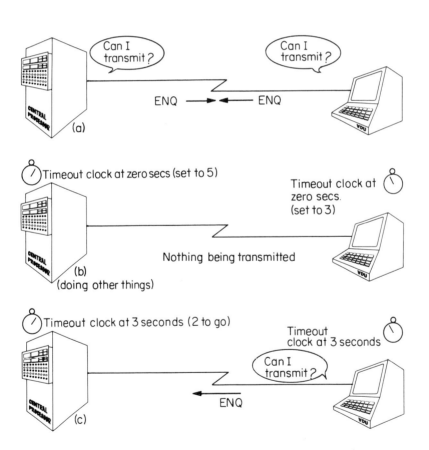

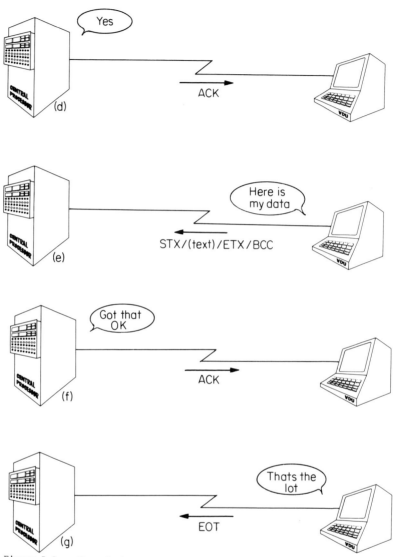

Figure 5.6.   Use of timeout in contention mode

5.11   CONVERSATIONAL

Conversational protocol is a form of point-to-point which is somewhat more 'streamlined'. Once the conversation has started, the number of control characters sent is reduced. This is done mainly by accepting a received text message as being a positive acknowledgement to the last transmitted block (Figure 5.7). In some cases it might be necessary to extend the protocol so that each message block contains some indication as to whether it is the last or merely an intermediate.

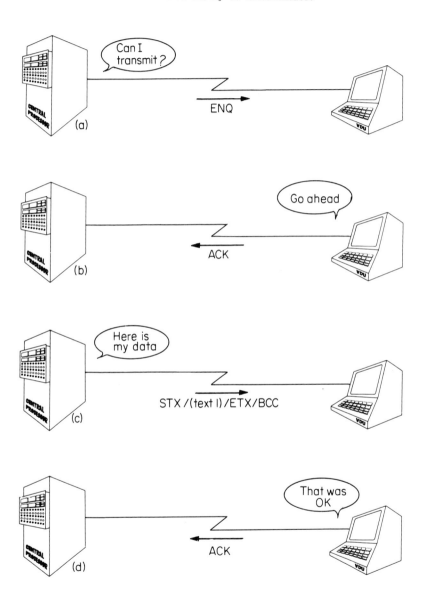

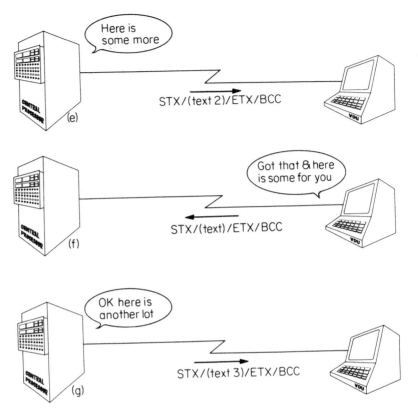

Figure 5.7.   Conversational line protocol

5.12   MULTIPOINT PROTOCOL

The protocol required for a multipoint circuit is analogous to the rules for the conduct of meetings. To prevent the proceeding from being reduced to an incoherent babel someone needs to be in charge; to decide who is going to speak and when. In data communications, this job of chairman invariably falls to the computer, primarily because of the complexity of the task. (The trick is to conduct the whole business much more efficiently than the average committee meeting!)

Each device attached to a circuit must have wired (or programmed) into it a unique 'address' one or two characters. Where a group of terminals are interfaced to the modem through a controller, the controller will have a 'main address' and the devices attached will have 'sub addresses

72

or 'device addresses'. The interface circuitry will 'listen' to all
the addresses on the line but only respond to its own, ignoring the others.
It should also be able to generate its own address(es) for inclusion in
data blocks as a security measure. The addresses are normally set in
the terminal by an engineer at installation time according to the requirements of the programmers and/or systems designers. Multipoint protocol
involves two basic operations; polling and selecting (or addressing).

5.13 POLLING

The normal cycle of operation is based upon the 'polling' of each
device on the circuit. In other words, the computer asks each device
in turn whether it has any data to send. The terminal concerned may
then reply with the data or, if none is ready, to indicate this in some
way so that the computer can then poll the next device in the sequence
(Figure 5.8). The response timeout is used to avoid hold ups caused by
terminals which have failed or are not switched on.

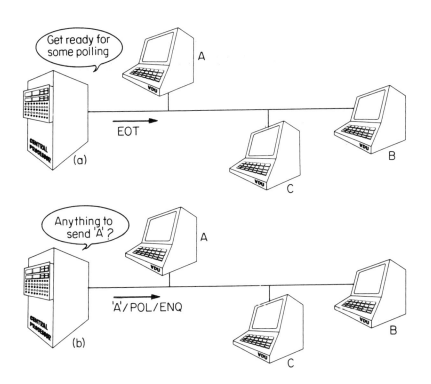

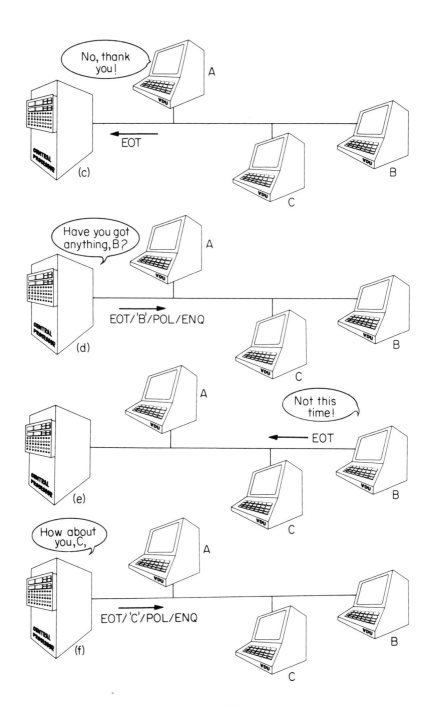

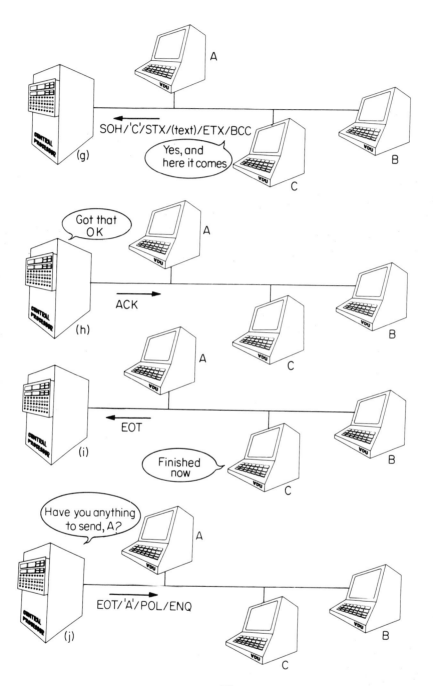

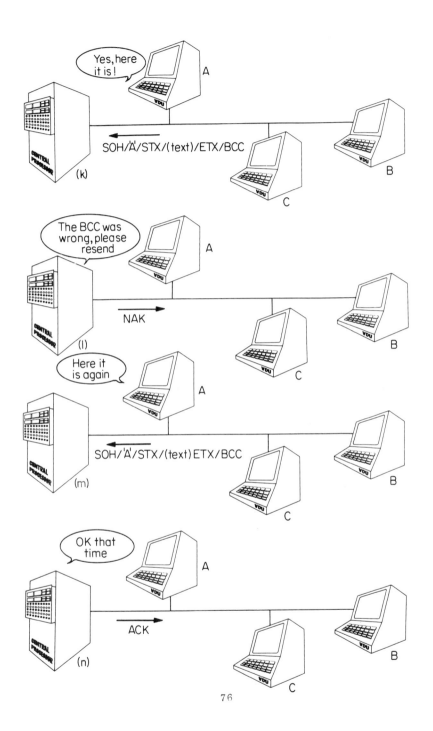

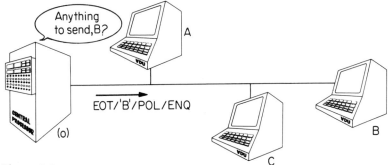

Figure 5.8.   Polling on a multipoint line

Where terminals are 'clustered' through a terminal controller two types of poll may be used. The first is a 'general poll' where the controller is asked if any of its devices have data for the CPU thus minimising the polling overhead on the line. If data is available, the controller inserts the device address so that the source can be identified exactly. The 'specific poll' is used where a particular terminal (whether clustered or not) is asked if it wishes to transmit.

In practice polling is even more complex than that shown in Figure 5.8. Examples of actual polling techniques are shown in Figures 5.9 and 5.10. The first is used to communicate with the Burroughs TC500 Programmable Hardcopy Terminal (*see* Chapter six) over asynchronous lines using the ASCII 7 bit code. The other example is of the procedure used by IBM for their 3270 stand-alone (or clustered) visual display terminals using synchronous transmission techniques and the 8 bit EBCDIC code. An extended version of the code is used and this is shown in Table 5.10.

Compare the different techniques used to avoid the loss of whole blocks of data. The IBM systems are based upon the use of a two character ACK: ACK0 and ACK1. ACK is used to confirm good receipt of all even numbered blocks (logically numbered that is), 0,2,4,6, etc., and ACK1 for odd numbered blocks. So if the transmitting device receives ACK1 followed by another ACK1 it knows that the last even block got lost somewhere.. Ah! But could it be that the last odd block was sent twice..! The TC500, being a programmable terminal can easily be a little bit more sophisticated and numbers each of its blocks sequentially from 0 to 999. Now there can be no doubt.   As the 3270 segments its data into 250-odd character blocks, it incorporates the facility to tell the computer that a block is only one of a series (ETB instead of ETX) that needs to be transmitted. Additional

77

pairs of SYN characters may be inserted automatically in the text as necessary to prevent the interface clocks going out of synchronism. These are stripped out by the hardware at each end.

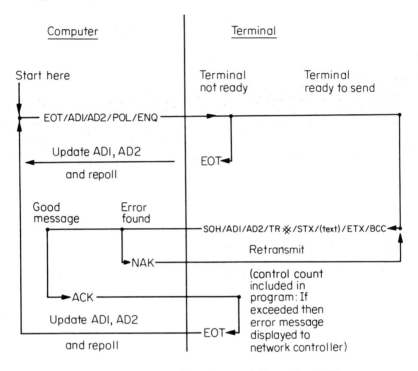

Figure 5.9. Polling example (asynchronous) Burroughs TC500

EOT	End of transmission
AD1	Two-character terminal address
AD2	
POL	ASCII lower case 'p': indicates poll operation
ENQ	Used to indicate that a response is required
SOH	Start of heading
TR#	Optional transmission number, up to three ASCII numerals
STX	Start of text
ETX	End of text
BCC	Block check character (longitudinal parity)
ACK	Acknowledgement
NAK	Negative acknowledgement

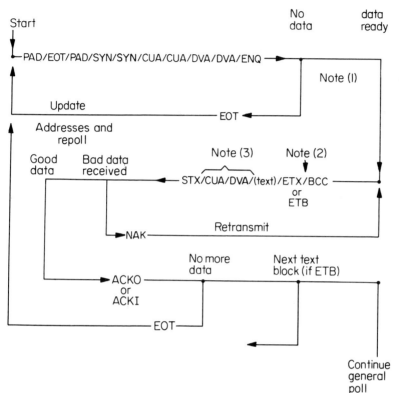

Figure 5.10. Polling example (synchronous) IBM 3270 information display system

PAD   Hardware generated one character time delay

EOT   End of transmission

SYN   Synchronous idle

CUA   Control unit address

DVA   Device address

ENQ   Response required

STX   Start of text

ETX   End of text

ETB   End of transmission block

BCC   Block checking character (3)

NAK   Negative acknowledgement

ACKO   Acknowledgement of even numbered text blocks

ACK1   Acknowledgement of odd numbered text blocks

Note (1):
See relevant IBM manuals for details of alternative responses

Note (2):
ETB is used instead of ETX when more blocks follow

Note (3):
Address need not be inserted after the first block

Table 5.10 *Extended EBCDIC code used by IBM 3270 system*

Bits 4567 ↓ / Hex 0 →	0	1	2	3	4	5	6	7	8	9	A	B	C	D	E	F
Bits 0,1 →	00	00	00	00	01	01	01	01	10	10	10	10	11	11	11	11
Bits 2,3 → (Hex 1)	00	01	10	11	00	01	10	11	00	01	10	11	00	01	10	11
0000 0	NUL	DLE			SP	&	·									0
0001 1	SOH	SBA				/			a	j			A	J		1
0010 2	STX	EUA		SYN					b	k	s		B	K	S	2
0011 3	ETX	IC							c	l	t		C	L	T	3
0100 4									d	m	u		D	M	U	4
0101 5	PT	NL							e	n	v		E	N	V	5
0110 6			ETB						f	o	w		F	O	W	6
0111 7			ESC	EOT					g	p	x		G	P	X	7
1000 8									h	q	y		H	Q	Y	8
1001 9		EM							i	r	z		I	R	Z	9
1010 A						!	¦	:								
1011 B					.	$	,	#								
1100 C		DUP		RA	<	*	%	@								
1101 D		SF	ENQ	NAK	(	)	_	'								
1110 E		FM			+	;	>	=								
1111 F		ITB		SUB			¬	?	"							

5.14   SELECTING (ADDRESSING)

'Selecting' is the technique used by the computer to determine the current status of a particular terminal with respect to its ability to receive a message. As most online systems are message-driven (i.e. an incoming message from a remote device initiates a processing cycle) selecting is normally used to send responses solicited by data obtained via the polling operation. In the case of a broadcasting system, the basic communications cycle would probably be a selecting sequence rather than a polling sequence. Figure 5.11 is an example of a message being sent from the computer in response to an input block. Note that it is not normally the case that the CPU can respond directly to the input without selecting. The reasons are :

(1) The time taken to generate the response might be so long that it is advisable to 'free' the line for other transmission.

(2) Immediately after transmitting the input message the tea-lady

80

trips over the mains cable and the terminal power goes down
(or some other failure occurs).

(3) The telephone line goes down.

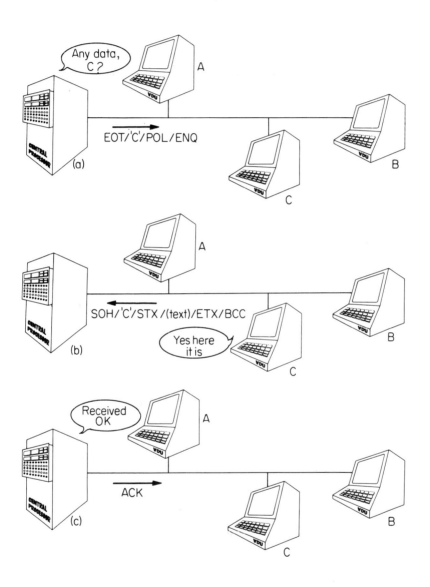

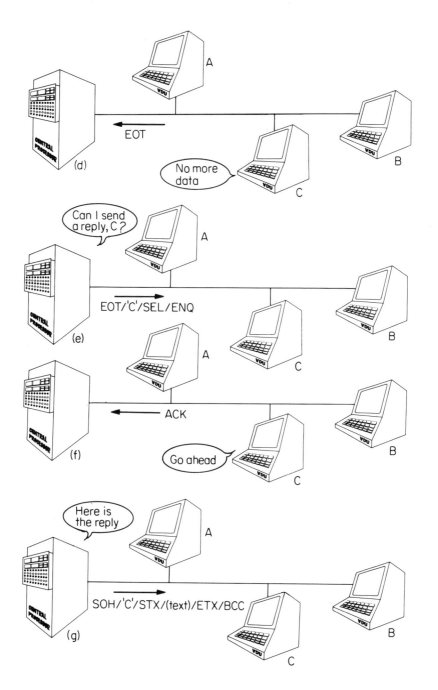

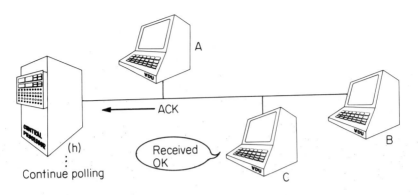

Figure 5.11. Selecting example (response to polled input)

Figure 5.12 shows an unsolicited selection breaking the polling sequence. The addressing techniques used on the TC500 and the 3270 are shown (in a simplified form) in Figure 5.13 and 5.14 respectively.

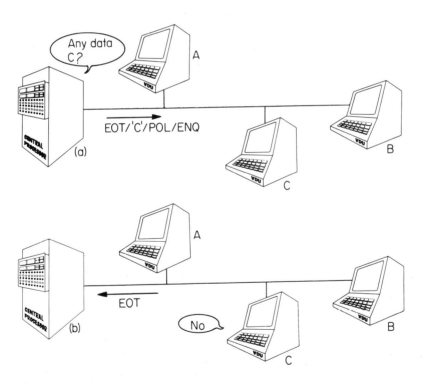

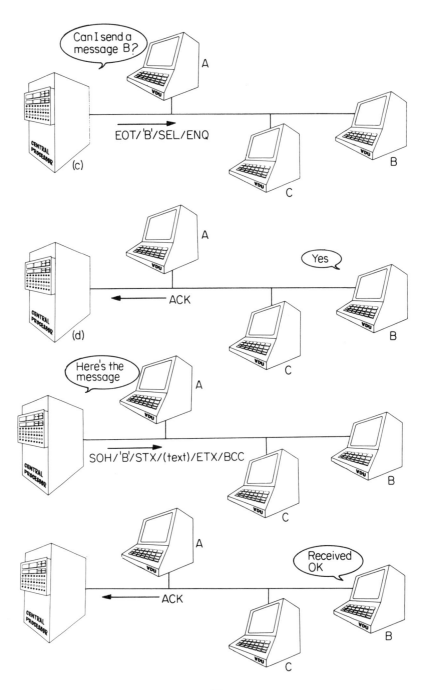

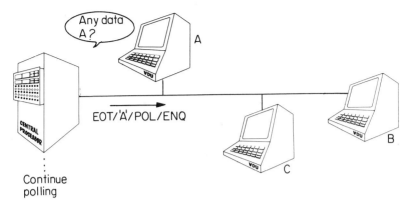

Figure 5.12. Selecting example (unsolicited transmission)

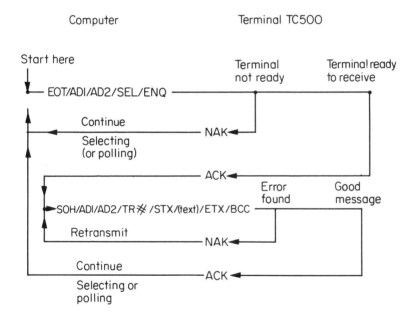

Figure 5.13. Selecting example (asynchronous) Burroughs TC500
              SEL   Select character (ASCII lower case 'q')
          Other characters as in Figure 5.9

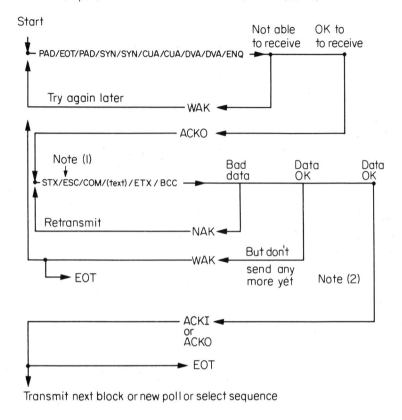

Figure 5.14. Selecting example (synchronous) IBM 3270 information
           display system
           WAK   Wait before transmit
           COM   3270 control unit command code
           ESC   Escape: always precedes the command code
           Other characters as in Figure 5.10
           Note (1): Example of the use of an escape code to
                     signify a special meaning to the following
                     one character
           Note (2): Although a block of text might be successfully
                     received, the completion of the operation might
                     be delayed (e.g. by a slow print operation)

The 3270 has a special control character (WAK) which means 'try again later'. This is mainly used when the serial printer associated with the VDU is still busy printing a previous block and it tells the CPU not to bother re-selecting straight away but to try again shortly (in, say, 3 sec). Other polling techniques are in use. One of them attempts to minimise the work that the CPU needs to do by having each terminal generate the poll characters for the next terminal in the sequence, if it has no data itself. This, of course, requires more expensive terminals and can lack flexibility. However, the basic approach described in this chapter is used almost universally.

QUESTIONS, DISCUSSION TOPICS AND ASSIGNMENTS

1. Describe five possible uses for 'escape' characters.

2. Apart from the number of bits used, what is the fundamental difference between CCITT IA No. 5 and EBCDIC from the viewpoint of data transmission?

3. Compare the benefits and disadvantages of fixed weight codes and parity checking. Why are hamming codes not widely used?

4. What are the two main types of 'timeout'? Why are timeouts necessary?

5. Is it possible to use contention protocol for multipoint lines? If not, why not?

6. Describe some situations where the selecting of a particular terminal might be unsolicited.

7. Take the example shown in Figure 5.11 and redraw it using Burroughs TC500 protocol and the convention used in Figures 5.9 and 5.13.

8. Consider the relative efficiencies of the polling systems used by the IBM 3270 and the Burrough TC500 and comment.

9. Obtain from a different manufacturer a manual describing the protocol used by one of their data transmission products and compare it with the devices mentioned in Question 8.

CHAPTER 6
TERMINALS

So far in this book we have concentrated on the way in which tele-communications facilities, both telephone and telegraph, can be utilised for the transmission of data. The design of modems, interfaces and line control procedures have also been described. In the next few chapters, a survey of the types of equipment which are available for data communications purposes will be made. Figure 6.1 shows the basic components which might occur in a teleprocessing system (though not necessarily all at once). These items are:

The Terminal
Multiplexors
Concentrators
Communications Control Units
The Central Processor

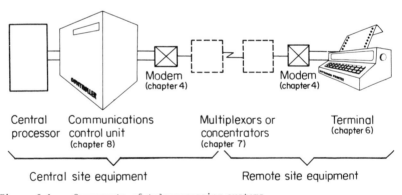

Figure 6.1.   Components of teleprocessing systems

This chapter will be concerned with terminals. Chapter 7 will describe devices used within the network; multiplexors and concentrators. Chapter

8 will discuss the functions of communications control units and the tasks
needed to be performed by the central processor in administering an online
network. Where particular devices are mentioned by name, this does not,
of course, imply a recommendation by the author.

6.1   CLASSIFICATION OF TERMINALS

There are undoubtedly many ways in which one can classify terminals;
by colour, weight, speed, price etc. The classification given here is
not necessarily going to meet the requirements of all interested parties.
It is, however, based on experience of what would be most useful (albeit
obvious) for the average potential commercial user.

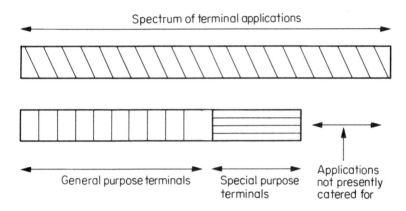

Figure 6.2.   Use of general or special purpose terminals

Figure 6.2 illustrates the extent to which general purpose terminals
might meet application needs. What cannot be met by such machines will
need to be fulfilled by special purpose devices. The proportion between
the two categories will obviously vary from supplier to supplier and the
exact split for the whole market cannot be certain. Indeed, it is the
policy of some manufacturers (e.g. IBM) to minimise the general purpose
product range and concentrate on obtaining large sectors of particular
markets by producing terminals specifically designed for that market.
Despite the fact that there are well over 200 terminals available in
Europe, there continues to be a number of applications for which suitable
terminals cannot be obtained (or, if they are available, then the price
is too high to make an online project feasible - which amounts to the
same thing).

Figure 6.3 takes this split between general and special purpose further by breaking the former into three sub-categories:

Batch

Interactive batch

Interactive

Even if the first and third terms are familiar, the second 'Interactive Batch' might not be. This is because the author recently 'invented' it to describe a fairly new range of devices which their salesmen were tending to call 'remote batch' and thereby confusing matters. A new term needed to be coined (not a popular thing to do in these days of 'instant dataspeak') but at least it does not use any new words!

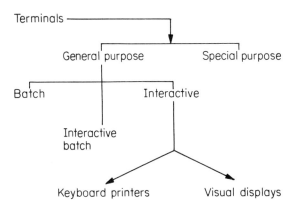

Figure 6.3. Categories of terminal devices

Figure 6.4 shows that batch operations involve two functionally separate machines. The first is a non-communications device for transcribing original documents into machine-readable form. This might be an orthodox card or paper tape punch or some kind of magnetic tape enscriber. The encoded medium is then transferred to a second machine, the terminal itself, for transmission to the computers. Interactive batch systems are becoming an increasingly important method of data capture. A device is used to transcribe data onto some magnetic medium, e.g. $\frac{1}{2}$ in magnetic tape, cassette tape, 'floppy' disc or 'rigid' disc. After the encoding phase, the data can be transmitted to the computer, but this is now done on the *same* device working in 'transmit' mode rather than 'input' mode.

True interactive working occurs when the data going to (or being received from) the computer does not go through any kind of intermediate storage, excluding the use of buffers. There are two major categories of interactive terminal:

Keyboard printer ('Hard copy')

Visual displays ('Soft copy')

These, and the batch units will be described in more detail later, but it might be useful to examine first of all the terminal's interface to the modem.

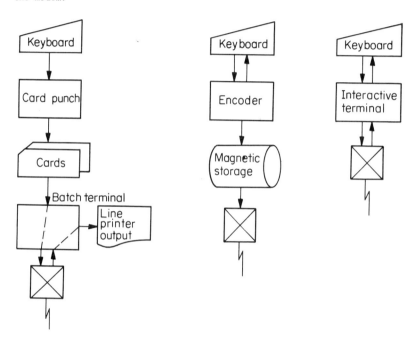

Figure 6.4.   Comparison of batch, interactive batch and interactive techniques

6.2   THE INTERFACE CONTROLLER

All types of terminal require some means of interfacing to the modem (or telegraph adaptor). What functions will this component need to be able to perform?

1. The serial-to-parallel and parallel-to-serial conversion of data (since data is treated as characters within the terminal and as bits on the line).

2. The insertion and deletion of start and stop bits *or* the insertion and deletion of SYN characters according to the

91

method of transmission timing being used.

3. The checking of data on a character or block basis.

4. The recognition and generation of control characters according to the protocol being used. The terminal will need to be able to identify, for example; EOT, ENQ, ETX and (if polled) its address characters. Similarly the interface logic must be able to generate, where required, such characters as ENQ, ACK, NAK, EOT and so on.

5. The logic for the 25 pin interface with the modem.

Typical sequences for the transmission and reception of a character are shown in Figures 6.5 and 6.6.

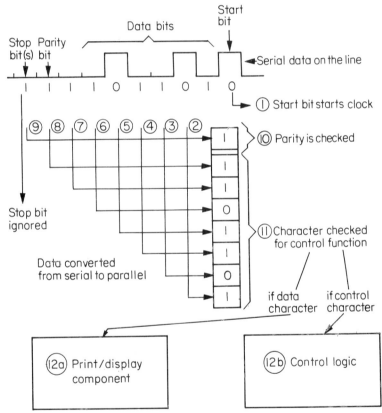

Figure 6.5.   Typical sequence for the reception of data from a line (asynchronous timing). Circled numbers indicate usual sequence of events

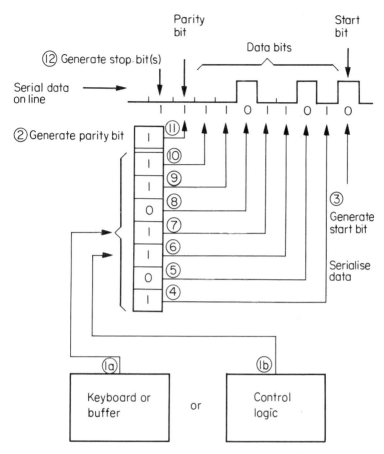

Figure 6.6.   Typical sequence (encircled numbers) for the transmission
of data to a line (asynchronous timing)

6.3   INTERACTIVE KEYBOARD PRINTERS

A keyboard printer, as its name implies, consists of three main
components:

1. An interface with the telecommunications facility being used
   (as described above).
2. A keyboard.
3. A printing mechanism.

The keyboard generally comprises three types of key:

1. A data key which will cause a character to print and be made available to the interface for transmission.
2. Keys for controlling the operation of the printer (CRLF, Back-space, etc.)
3. Keys for controlling the transmission of data (EOB, XMT, ATTN, etc.)

The printer is the area in which most development has taken place over the past few years with particular attention being paid to improvements in speed. The major characteristics of printers currently available are as follows (Table 6.1 summarises these details).

Table 6.1   *Some features of serial printers used in Terminals*

Platen widths	74, 80, 100, 120, 132 and 160 print positions (10 ch/inch horizontally and 6 ch/inch vertically)
Platen arrangements	Roll or 'fanfold' stationery. Friction feed or pin feed. 'Split' platen arrangements. Front feed forms shute
Stationery Control	Horizontal tabbing Vertical tabbing (forms alignment)
Printing mechanisms:	Printing speeds
Impact { Hammers	< 10 ch/sec
Cylinder	10 ch/sec
Sphere	15-20 ch/sec
Multiple cylinders	< 60 ch/sec
Circulating belt or chain	10-120 ch/sec
Matrix	180 ch/sec +
Non-impact { Thermal	< 60 ch/sec
Others	Up to 250 ch/sec

Platen width

The width of the printer platen in terms of the number of positions available (generally at 10 per inch) are:

74 print positions (the standard for teleprinters)

80 print positions (to correspond to a standard punch card and a common width of VDUs.)

100 print positions

94

$$\left.\begin{array}{c}120\\132\\160\end{array}\right\}$$ Widths available on computer line printers.

Platen types

Paper can be fed through the printer from a roll or from 'fanfold' continuous stationery. The paper may be pulled through by pins or by friction rollers. Also platens may be 'split' so that two (or more) different sets of stationery may be used on some applications. Loose sheets of paper (or savings passbooks) may be inserted in the printer via a 'front feed forms shute'.

Printing techniques

There are two categories here: impact and non-impact. Until some years ago almost all serial printers used impact printing mechanisms with the characters embossed on hammers (as in a typewriter), spheres (as the IBM 'Golfball'), cylinders (as on the Teletype). Speeds available were usually 6·6, 10 or 15 ch/sec. In order to improve on this a number of companies, notably NCR, developed printers which used a matrix of electrically heated pins to form a character by touching heat sensitive paper. Other devices used a similar matrix head to strike a special ink impregnated paper thus causing a character to appear. These techniques gave speeds of up to 30 ch/sec. More recently, efforts have concentrated on developing impact techniques in order to overcome the deficiencies of non-impact methods, namely the cost of the paper and the lack of copies. It has proved to be very difficult to produce whole character impact printers that will give a high quality impression at 30 ch/sec and over. Consequently the higher speeds of up to 180 ch/sec have been achieved using matrix impact mechanisms. These produce a good impression (including lower case) but some users do object to the fact that the print does not look like that from a typewriter. Other 'off beat' terminals have been produced which achieve even higher speeds e.g. the Inktronic and A.B. Dick's Videojet 9600, both at reasonable prices.

Keyboard/printer

Figure 6.7 shows the three main configurations of keyboard/printer in use. The simplest has a direct interface with the line; press a key and a character is transmitted and printed at the same time. The 'original' terminal was probably the Teletype, the American version of our teleprinte and originally devised for use on the US Switched telegraph service TWX (pronounced 'twix'); Teletypewriter Exchange. Because of the volumes produced, the price became very low (c.£600) and it has undoubtedly become the most widely installed terminal in the world, particularly with the time-sharing services. The teletype uses a cylinder print head which gives nondescript quality at 10 ch/sec. It has three modes of operation as shown in Figure 6.8. Three arrangments of unit are available:

RO   Read (i.e. print) only
KSR   Keyboard Send/Receive
ASR   KSR + paper tape punch and reader

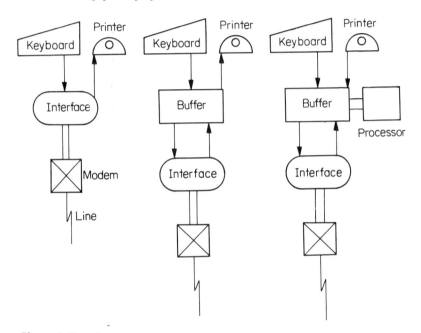

Figure 6.7.   Interactive keyboard/printer arrangements

The '33' model is the basic form, the '35' and '38' giving higher relia-bility and higher speed respectively. Many terminals have been designed to beat the teletype in terms of speed, but few have beaten it in terms of price.

The teletype in its standard version is not capable of recognising poll characters, but some US companies have developed 'stunt' boxes which sit between the teletype and give it this capability. IBM's standard keyboard/printer is the 2740 range which is based upon the 15 ch/sec 'golfball' Selectric typewriter. The 2741 is a contention

96

device mainly for time sharing use. The 2740 I is pollable and may, therefore, be multidropped.

The 2740 II is essentially the same as the 2740 I but is *buffered*. In order to overcome the disadvantage of having to restrict the utili- sation of a multidrop line by the keying speed of the terminal operators, a variable size buffer is placed between the keyboard and the line inter- face. The two methods of working may be contrasted from the operators point of view, as follows:

| *Unbuffered* | *Buffered* |

1. Press ATTN key for line   1. Obtain buffer (keyboard unlocks)
2. When next polled, keyboard   2. Key data into buffer
   unlocks
3. Operator keys data for a   3. Press ATTN key for line.
   variable period of time   4. When next polled, the interface
                                                  transmits the buffer contents
                                                  at maximum line speed.

Such buffers (which may be core or IC chips) obviously add to the cost of the terminal, but such additional costs might be recovered from the savings incurred in line rental by increased multidropping. Some key- board/printers are now available which contain processors and can act as small computers in their own right. The most widely installed device of this type is the Burroughs TC500, of which more than 8,000 have been installed by the U.K. clearing banks. The TC500's storage is a small fixed-head disc on which both data and instructions can be held. 'Firmware' or 'micro-programmed' logic is used to effect the interface with the modem.

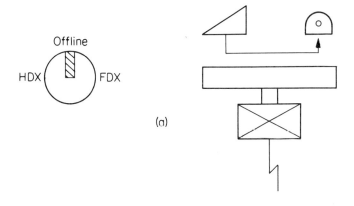

(a)

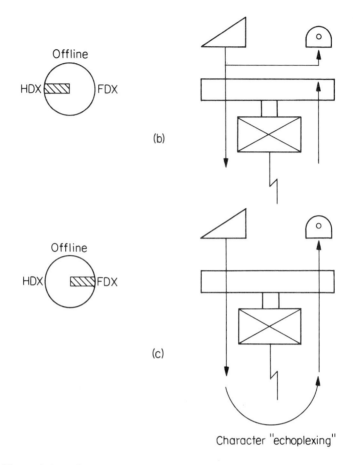

Offline

HDX ▨ FDX

(b)

Offline

HDX ▨ FDX

(c)

Character "echoplexing"

Figure 6.8.   Teletype modes of operation
    (a)   No transmission, keyboard directly connected
        to the printer
    (b)   As key is pressed, printer operates and character
        is transmitted. Received character goes directly
        to the printer
    (c)   No direct connection with the keyboard. As the
        key is depressed a character is transmitted and
        the CPU hardware/software transmits it back for
        printing as a verification

Programs are written in a form of assembler and even a COBOL compiler
is available. Another similar device in extensive use in Europe is the
Nixdorf programmable terminals which are micro-programmed using 'wire
wrap' firmware logic.

There are many peripheral devices which can be attached to hard-copy
terminals in order to enhance their capabilities (Figure 6.9). Paper
tape readers and punches are most commonly available because this has
traditionally been the medium for telecommunications. Certainly the
devices themselves are inexpensive and have a relatively high degree
of reliability. Inevitably, some terminals can read and/or punch cards
but this is relatively uncommon on less sophisticated interactive terminals.

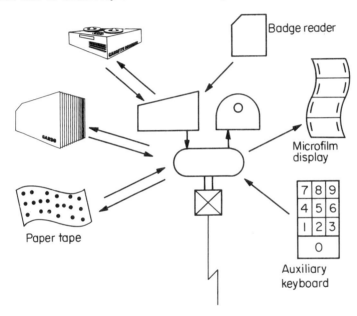

Figure 6.9.   'Peripherals' for keyboard printers

The use of cassetted magnetic tape is becoming extremely popular. Although
the reading/recording device is slightly more expensive than paper tape
units (but not very much more in view of the fact that the recorders are
based upon a 'mass' technology) there are other advantages: the cassettes
are compact and easy to handle, they can be 'scanned' and are probably
cheaper than paper tape because of the higher recording density and the
fact that they can be reused.

Badge readers are often incorporated on an optional basis as a security feature. The cheapest form of badge is like a small piece of Hollerith encoded punched card.

At least one manufacturer (IBM) has developed a terminal (the 2760) which includes a 16 mm microfilm projector which can be controlled from the computer. The projector screen has a matrix of light-sensitive spots which can be 'activated' with a light-pen thus enabling the unit to be used for input as well as output. The cost of this device might inhibit its use in many beneficial areas, but if more manufacturers produce such terminals and the price comes down, many more will be installed for advanced information retrieval applications.

6.4   VISUAL DISPLAY UNITS

Visual display units (VDUs) are becoming increasingly popular as general purpose terminals (Figure 6.10). This is probably because, compared with serial printer, they are pleasant and easy to operate. The main components of such a terminal are:

A keyboard
A buffer store
A character generator
A display
A modem interface

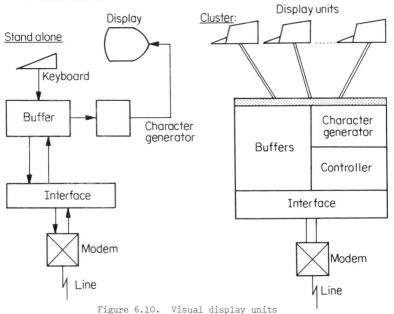

Figure 6.10.   Visual display units

100

Visual displays may be 'stand alone' units where one integral keyboard and screen unit interface to a modem. Alternatively the device might be 'clustered' which means that much of the common control circuitry (and buffering) is shared by the displays and placed in one cabinet. Only one modem interface is generally used. This technique is intended to minimise overall costs when lots of terminals are installed in one location. Stand-alone displays can still use one of the modem-sharing devices described in Chapter 4.

The vast majority of VDUs currently in use, incorporate a television type cathode ray tube (CRT) on the face of which information can be displayed. The main components of the CRT are shown in Figure 6.11.

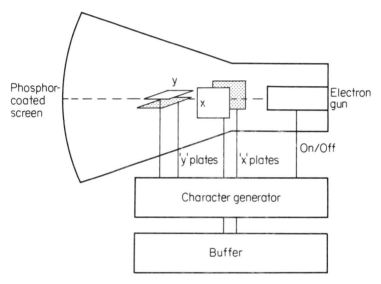

Figure 6.11. Cathode ray tube display

At the rear of the CRT an 'electron gun' produces a beam of electrons which eventually strike the face of the tube. This face is coated with a phosphor which emits light when hit by the electron beam. In order to form characters on the screen the generator can move the beam by applying voltages to 'X' and 'Y' plates which, in turn cause the beam to deflect to the required part of the screen. The beam can also be switched on and off. Because the phosphor begins to fade immediately the beams stop hitting a particular point, it is necessary for the 'picture' of data on the screen to be continually 'refreshed'; normally at a rate of 50 or 60 Hz. Hence the requirement for the buffer.

101

The ICL Termiprinter is an unbuffered serial keyboard printer which
can operate at 10 or 30 ch/sec. *Courtesy of ICL*

The Teletype is still the most widely used terminal. Shown here is
the 10 ch/sec ASR-33 version with the paper tape reader and punch
at the left of the device. *Photograph by the author*

The French-made Logabax LX-180 is an impact matrix printer which will operate at up to 180 ch/sec and is buffered to the line. The model shown here is a 'read only' version for use where input is not required. *Courtesy Computer & Systems Engineering Ltd.*

The IBM 3735 Programmable Buffered Terminal is based upon a much modified version of the 'Selectric' typewriter which uses a 'golfball' print mechanism. A speed of up to 15 ch/sec is possible but an alternative 40 ch/sec matrix printer is available. *Courtesy IBM United Kingdom Ltd.*

This picture of the powerful TC.3500 programmable terminal shows the wide range of 'peripherals' which can often be attached to such devices; a ledger feed, cassette tapes, a display screen, line printer and $\frac{1}{2}$" magnetic tape. The terminal may be programmed in COBOL. *Courtesy Burroughs Machines Ltd.*

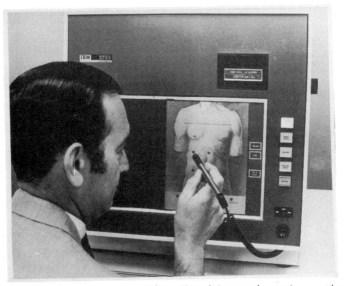

The IBM 2780 Optical Image Unit. The light pen is used to activate one of a number of light sensitive points on the screen of the microfilm projector. See text. *Courtesy IBM United Kingdom Ltd.*

```
(DACT/33053462017/01                                    PAGE 1 OF 2

ATLAS ENGINEERING LTD          404 PURLEY WAY
TARIFF   T06                                    PMTS 03.10          302.57
P/S     6.70       STAT 010 010 100 000              18.08          294.16
MRD DUE 10.12      D/BAL      22.76                   29.04          378.81

                        - CURRENT BILL 28.09.71 -

142 048762M 043216M             2773.0
301 000024M 009136M              444.0
210 006731M 006711M               10.0
765 000134M 000134M
412 009673M 009531M               71.0
124 000010M 000000C                5.0
642 046213C 046213M
465 054361M 004199M               81.0CR
333 000341M 000097M                               122.0 CHK
346 009346M 009346M
TOTAL THERMS                    3222.0
                                 100.0a 14.000       14.00
                                 400.0a  9.500       38.00
BALANCE C/FWD                  27722.0_
  .
```

Example of a screen of data produced using a cathode ray tube and
a 5 × 7 matrix character generation technique. *Courtesy Sanders
Data Systems Ltd.*

A teletype compatible VDU. Five simple cursor movement keys may be
seen at the right of the keyboard. *Courtesy Computer & Systems
Engineering Ltd.*

Many techniques have been used to form the characters on the screen, but the most popular system at the moment is the dot matrix. The number of dots used for each character depends upon the degree of definition required; 5 by 7 is common and 7 by 9 is occurring more frequently. An advantage of this approach is that the characters can be formed by 'scanning' the screen in the same way that a picture is formed on a domestic television set. The beam is passed across the screen 625 times, its strength being varied to give degrees of shade. For the 'return' from the end of one line to the beginning of the next, the beam is turned off. Visual Displays do the same thing but the beam is switched on and off to produce the dots of the matrix (Figure 6.12).

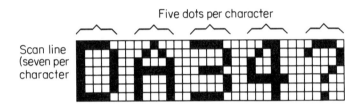

Figure 6.12.   CRT character generation using 5 × 7 dot matrix.
Characters normally appear on screens white, blue
or green on black depending on the phosphor used.

One of the major economic advantages of the 'TV compatible' approach is that standard low-cost components may be used in the manufacture of the terminal. Also the character generator output can be fed into any domestic television set or commercial monitor to produce a picture. Most displays have a 'one for one' correspondence between the buffer and the screen. Some units vary from this by having buffers which are smaller than the screen or buffers which are larger. The former works on the basis that it is unnecessary to store the many 'blank' positions which appear on the screen and so only displayed data is stored in the buffer, each item being preceded by details of its location. The second approach works on the basis that it will often be convenient to store more data in the terminal than needs to be displayed at any one time. The operator can then 'page' through the data as required, the screen acting as a 'window' to the buffer. Some more sophisticated VDUs are able to offer 'split screen' facilities effectively giving two separate displays on which different dialogues can take place.

Typical screen dimensions for CRT based terminals are shown in Figure

6.13. Two manufacturers have recently announced displays based upon 'Self-scan' screens developed by Burroughs. The screens are simply a matrix of neon-type lamps which are illuminated in combination to form the characters required. The data is stored within the display panel itself, thereby eliminating the need for a separate buffer store. The panels are flat (1 or 2 in thick) and very easy to read.

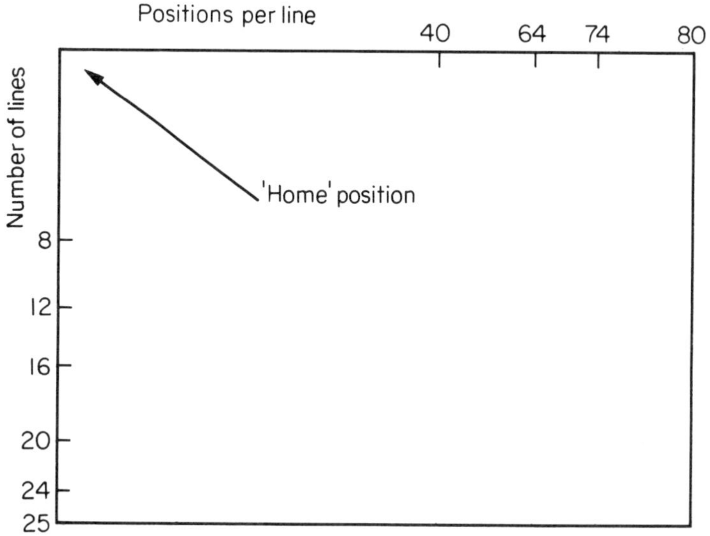

Figure 6.13. Typical dimensions of VDU screens

On a VDU, when the operator presses a key, the data enters a buffer and from there it is reproduced onto the screen. But no data has been transmitted until the 'SEND' or 'TRANSMIT' key has been depressed. When a character of data is received from the line, it goes into the buffer and immediately appears on the screen. Therefore, although VDUs are keyboard buffered they are not buffered on the output side. How does the operator know, if a key is pressed, where the corresponding character will appear on the screen? This is done through a device called a CURSOR which usually appears on the screen as an underline to the position into which the next character will be entered. Other cursors appear as ⊔, |||, ☰ and reverse video. If a key *is* pressed then the cursor will automatically move to the next position to the right on the same line of the screen. If the cursor was originally at the last position on the line it will move to the first position on the next line down. If the cursor was at the last position of all on the screen, entering a character will cause the cursor to move to the first position on the screen (known as the 'home' position) (*see* Figure 6.14). The cursor may blink on and off in order to make it easier to locate.

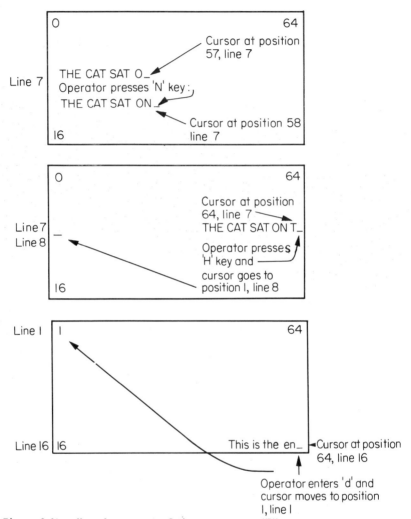

Figure 6.14. Normal movement of the cursor on a VDU

VDU keyboards incorporate a number of keys for the control of the cursor, although not all functions will be available on every terminal (Figure 6.15). (Note that cursor movements do not affect the contents of the positions concerned.) The functions performed are as follows:-

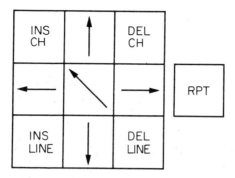

Figure 6.15. VDU cursor control keys

Causes the cursor to move one position to the
← left (backspace).

↑ Causes the cursor to move up to the same
position on the previous line.

Causes the cursor to move one position
→ to the right.

↓ Causes the cursor to move down to the same position
on the next line.

(All the above operations will 'wrap' around a line
or screen depending upon the original position of
the cursor.)

↖ Home cursor. Moves the cursor to the first position
on the first line.

INS CH.   This (and the next three keys) lock down or need
            to be held depressed. When a data key is pressed
            all positions to the right of the cursor (including
            its own) move one position to the right and the
            character is inserted at the cursor position. A
            character may be lost off the end of the line (no
            wrap occurs).

DEL CH.   Delete character. Works the opposite way from
            insert character.

INS LINE   Insert line. Inserts from the current cursor
            position one line of blanks (e.g. 80 characters)
            moving all other data down the screen.

DEL LINE   Delete Line. Works the opposite way from insert
            line.

109

RPT   Repeat. Causes the operation selected to repeat
             continually until the key is released.

There are two basic types of VDU in use:

    Teletype compatible

    Commercial

The main features of each are contrasted in Table 6.2.

Table 6.2   *Characteristics of Visual Displays*

Teletype	*Commercial*
Low cost	Medium to high cost
Scrolling	Forms mode input
Limited cursor control	Full cursor control
Character transmission	Selective transmission
Point-to-point only	Lower case, italics, blink etc.
	Function keys and selection systems
	Dot graphics
	Good choice of peripherals
	May be programmable
	Multidropping possible

Teletype compatible displays were developed as low cost plug-for-plug
replacements for standard hard copy teletypes. Prices vary from £400
to £1200 according to the facilities incorporated. Cursor control
features are usually limited (no insertion or deletion) and the method
of using the screen resembles the use of continuous stationery. 'Scrol-
ling' occurs when the screen becomes full of the interactive conversation
between the operator and the computer. As new lines are needed the whole
screen is moved up one line to generate a blank at the bottom and pushing
the first line off the top. Note that, although the terminal will be
fully buffered, transmission will take place on a character-by-character
basis in order to emulate the normal modes of the teletype (Figure 6.8).

    Commercial displays are designed for the general purpose market and
are normally much more powerful (and expensive) than the 'teletype'
displays. However the major difference lies in the use of a particular
way of using the screen to enter data. This technique has been given
many names but, for reasons which will become obvious, the term 'forms
mode' will be used.

110

Forms mode is based upon three cursor control keys and characters
thus:

TAB

[Tab stop

] Auto tab

The TAB key causes the cursor to move to the next 'tab stop' display
on the screen. If the cursor is moved, by any means, so that it is in
position at an 'autotab' character it is automatically 'tabbed' to the
next tab stop. (It must be mentioned that not all terminals display the
tab stop and autotab characters as shown above. Some use different shapes,
e.g. 6 and 9 and others use dots to indicate the field between the brackets).
The tab stop and autotab characters are used to 'bracket' fields which
are to be entered from the keyboard.

Figure 6.16 shows a screen set-up for the entry of a customer's order.
The content will have been transmitted as a message from the CPU at the
request of an operator. The shading is included for reasons of clarity
only.

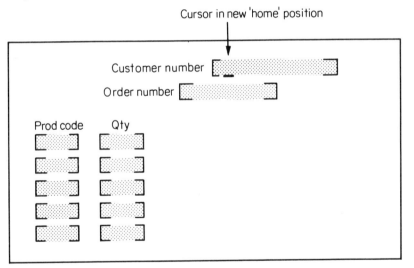

Cursor in new 'home' position

Figure 6.16. Forms mode VDU screen (see Figure 6.17 for completed
version)

In forms mode the home position for the cursor becomes the position
to the left of the first tab stop. This is the first position of the
'customer number' field in our example. The operator follows this sequence

in entering the data:

1. Key a fixed length 8 digit customer number.
2. The eighth key depression will take the cursor to the autotab character and thence to the first position of the 'order number' field.

(Note that heading 'Order number' is protected from possible corruption. If the backspace key (←) is pressed then the cursor will go back to the 'customer number' field).

3. The variable length order number is keyed. If this is less than the 10 positions allocated then the operator will have to press the TAB key to get the cursor to the first product code field.
4. The variable length quantity is entered and TAB is used to get to the next line.
5. Steps 3 and 4 are repeated until all order items have been entered.
6. Press the 'SEND' or 'TRANSMIT' key causing all the *variable* data (i.e. that in brackets) to be sent down the line.
7. A key is usually available for the clearing of variable fields prior to the entry of the next order (or whatever). This should be distinguished from a control key which will clear the whole screen.

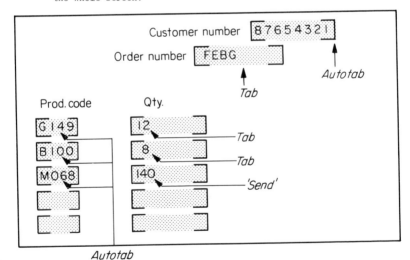

Figure 6.17. Forms mode VDU screen (completed input)

The advantages of forms mode are:

1. Ease of operation
2. Protection of headings and 'fixed' information.
3. Transmission of variable data only.

Some terminals (e.g. the Swedish ITT Alfaskope) have multilevel tabbing. This would enable tabs to be carried out *within* fields as well as from one field to the next. Programmable displays can provide almost unlimited possibilities with respect to forms mode data entry. Commercial displays usually have a full range of cursor control functions, most of which will operate within the scope of forms mode operation. Options with respect to displayable characters are increasingly extensive with such items as lower case, italics, reverse video (i.e. black on white instead of white on black), the ability to make portions of the screen blink on and off and, last but not least, the use of colour. Also, many TV compatible terminals provide facilities for limited graphics use by means of using the whole screen (or portions of it) as one big dot matrix. In order to simplify the operation of the terminal, suppliers are providing function keys with their VDUs. These come in a number of different versions:

1. Keys which send a special control character to the program to request a particular operation (without any data from the screen).
2. Keys which do the same as (1) but do send any data which might be on the screen.
3. Keys which do the same as (1) but are positioned adjacent to the screen so that meanings might be allocated dynamically (Figure 6.18).

Related to function keys are other types of selection systems.

4. The light pen. This is a device which does not produce light. In fact, when touched to the CRT screen, attracts the electron beam enabling the control circuitry to 'read' from the X and Y plates the position of the pen on the screen. The pen can thus be used to select items from a list on the display.
5. The light matrix. This is an ingenious and inexpensive system comprising rows of light sources on two (adjacent) sides of the screen. Opposite each lamp is a photo-electric cell (Figure 6.19). Any object (e.g. a finger) placed close to the screen will cause two beams to be broken thereby

113

providing the terminal with co-ordinates it can send to the CPU. The meaning of the selection will, of course, be dependent upon the current screen content.

6. Touch-wires. The U.K. company Ferranti, have developed a system whereby a grid of short, almost invisible wires is placed over all or part of the screen. The depression of one of the wires causes the completion of an electrical circuit and thence a particular value to be sent to the computer. Again, the meaning will depend upon the programming of the dialogue between the operator and the system, but much scope exists (as with 4 and 5) for imaginative use.

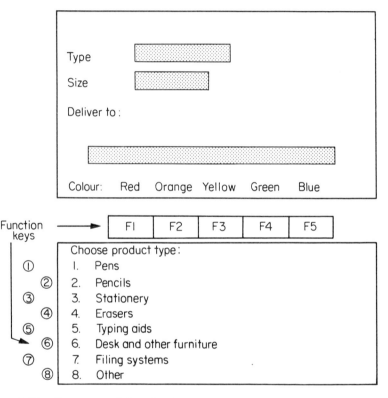

Figure 6.18. Two types of function key

The incorporation of mini or micro-computers in terminals has been done much more extensively in VDUs than in keyboard/printers. One of the most widely used terminals in airline reservations, is such a display manufactured by Incoterm Inc. The advantages of such a programmable device are threefold:

1. Local processing capability improves the response time of the 'dialogue' and increases the quality of data sent to the CPU.

2. Improves the efficiency of transmission through data compression techniques and the elimination of low level (e.g. syntactical) errors.

3. Facilitates the emulation of other terminals in order to simplify the problems of interfacing to an 'alien' mainframe.

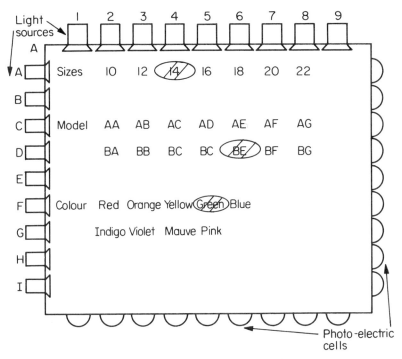

Figure 6.19. Use of a light matrix for selection input on a VDU screen. If the input was for size 14, model BE in green, each of these is pointed ot on the screen in turn causing beams A4, D6 and F5 respectively to break

Visual display units probably have a wider range of peripherals than

115

hard copy terminals (Figure 6.20). Paper tape is generally available
on teletype compatible CRTs for the same reasons that it is available
on teletypes. Card peripherals are not very common but do occur on more
powerful, usually programmable terminals for occasional bulk transmission
and for program loading. However, most programmable terminals have one
or two integral cassette recorders. These are required for program
loading but can provide useful facilities for the local entry of data
prior to transmission (perhaps on a dialled line) at a later time. One
tape can be used to hold the input screen formats and the other can be
used to hold the data that is keyed.

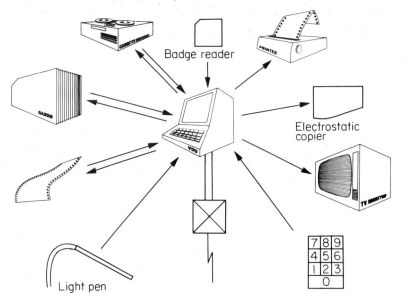

Figure 6.20. 'Peripherals' for VDUs

As with keyboard/printers it is becoming easier to obtain displays
with security features such as badge readers and locks. In spite of the
obvious attractions of the VDU and the systems man's 'paperless society',
there is still a major requirement for paper in many applications. This
in itself can impose restrictions on the way in which the display is used
unless the printer is of reasonably adequate speed. Most of the serial
printers described earlier in the chapter are available in a Read Only
version for attachment directly to the teletype output socket which most
displays are delivered with as standard.

116

Some attempts have been made to achieve even greater speeds. The SE
Data Product's Statprinter can produce a copy from a screen in less than
3 sec. One model of the Statprinter has a dial which can be set to produce
up to 10 copies at one go. Unfortunately, special paper needs to be used
thereby making it difficult to print onto a company's individual stationery.

Displays which are TV compatible can output video signals on a standard
co-axial cable to domestic sets or commercial monitors. This enables large
size copies of the screen to be made visible to users of the system other
than the terminal operator. Indeed monitors with video output sockets can
be 'daisy-chained' to provide a whole series of 'slave' displays costing
less than £200 each - an inexpensive way of providing an information broadcasting service. (Figure 6.21). Some teletype compatible devices use TV
sets or monitors instead of an integral CRT.

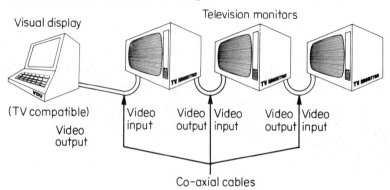

Figure 6.21. Use of 'slave' television monitors

6.5   INTERACTIVE BATCH DEVICES

The phrase 'interactive batch' is used to describe devices where the
input keying operation is interactive but transmission to the computer
is in batch mode. Data is initially keyed onto some kind of magnetic
storage medium which may be incorporated within the terminal or may be
interchangeable. Examples of the storage used:

    Fixed-head disc
    Cassette tape
    Cartridge tape   Removable
    Industry compatible tape ($\frac{1}{2}$in)
    'Floppy' disc

The criteria that the encoding and the transmission should take place on
the same device does not apply 100%, but where the functions are separate

117

the whole operation is generally designed as an integrated function
(e.g. IBM's 3740).

The simplest (and currently most popular) interactive batch terminal
comprises a keyboard, a display (which may range from a set of numeric
nixie tubes to a full CRT) and a cassette tape or $\frac{1}{2}$ inch magnetic tape
encoder (Figure 6.22). In the 'input' mode the operator keys the data
onto the tape, perhaps rekeying to perform some kind of verification.
At the end of the day, or at intervals throughout the day, the terminal
can be put online (probably on the public switched telephone network)
and the tape or tapes can be transmitted. There is no output capability.

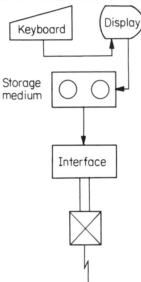

Figure 6.22. Interactive batch tape encoder

IBM recently announced a new data input device (the 3740) for encoding
'Diskettes' or 'floppy' discs. Because of their high recording density
and ruggedness, these discs can be mailed at fairly low postal rates from
locations where the amount of data being originated does not justify online
working. Where volumes are high enough, an online diskette reader can be
installed (Figure 6.23). All encoded discs can be collected together and
loaded into the reader which will transmit the contents over a line, again
probably dialled. There are no output facilities. For locations where
volumes are extremely high, a company might wish to install one of the
cluster key-to-tape or key-to-disc systems which have become very popular
recently as replacements for traditional card-punching installations

(Figure 6.24). Most of these systems are based upon minicomputers and can easily be given communications capability. It may, in some instances, be possible to fit a printer to the minibased controller so that output reports can be sent back to the remote location.

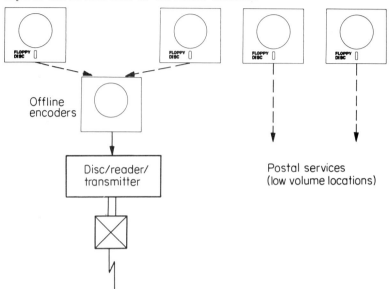

Figure 6.23. Disc encoders with batch transmission facilities

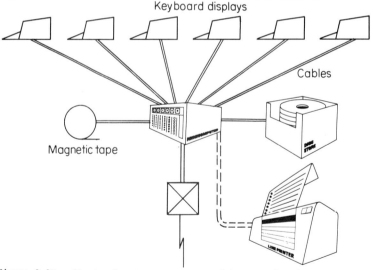

Figure 6.24. Cluster key to tape system with communications capability

The IBM 3735 is one of the more sophisticated terminals designed for interactive batch working. It is a programmable device with its own high level programming language. Programs and data are stored on an inbuilt fixed head disc. The device (Figure 6.25) has three modes of operation:

Local working with the disc
Transmission of input
Reception of output

Each is quite a separate function and cannot be overlapped. A typical sequence is as follows:

1. Order details are keyed into the terminal verified by the program and recorded on the disc. Details of any errors are shown on the printer.
2. A line is dialled to the computer centre and the input data file is transmitted to the CPU.
3. Either immediately, or at some later time, the computer sends back completed delivery notes which are recorded on the disc.
4. Once off-line the operator can cause the delivery notes to be printed out on preprinted stationery (at 15 or 40 ch/sec).

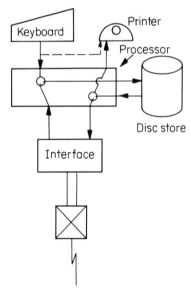

Figure 6.25. Programmable interactive batch terminal

120

A programmable VDU, the Sanders 804 used in an order entry application.
An order document is displayed on the screen using 'forms mode' techniques
(see text). The variable items to be entered by the operator are
represented by dots. *Courtesy Sanders Data Systems Ltd.*

The ICL 7181 VDU is a non programmable commercial display and is
shown here with a 'read only' Termiprinter for producing hardcopy
and a paper tape reader. *Courtesy ICL.*

The IBM 3270 is a sophisticated display system which can be supplied
in a 'cluster' or 'stand alone' configuration. It is seen here with a
small screen of 480 characters and a special purpose printing device
for use in the financial area (5914). *Courtesy IBM United Kingdom Ltd.*

The Incoterm VDU is a general purpose stand alone terminal which incorporates its own minicomputer and has been widely installed by the airlines. *Courtesy Incoterm Ltd.*

As with programmable hard copy terminals, intelligent VDUs can be
expanded to remote batch configurations by the attachment of peripherals
like the card reader and line printer shown with this Sanders 810.
Courtesy Sanders Data Systems Ltd.

The CASE GTU is an interactive batch device. The data is keyed onto
the screen in 'forms mode' for visual checking and then transcribed
onto one of the standard cassettes shown above the keyboard. Two
cassette drives are incorporated so that a verifying function can take
place. Finally, the data can be transmitted to the computer from the
cassette over a dialled line. *Courtesy Computer & Systems Engineering Ltd.*

Remote batch terminals are used for the bulk input and output of data, sometimes using paper tape but overwhelmingly through 80 column punched cards. Output is to a line printer or a very fast serial printer. Traditionally, the input-output devices used are the slower speed peripherals used for the manufacturers central site computer configurations. These are interfaced to the line through a hard-wired controller. A typical configuration might be:

Controller
Card reader (150 cpm)
Card punch (50 cpm)
Line printer (250 lpm)
 and (optionally)
Console typewriter

Modes of operation are relatively simple; transmit cards, punch cards or print listings. Limited off-line capability such as the ability to list cards might be available. Such systems can cost anywhere between £15,000 and £30,000 (Figure 6.26).

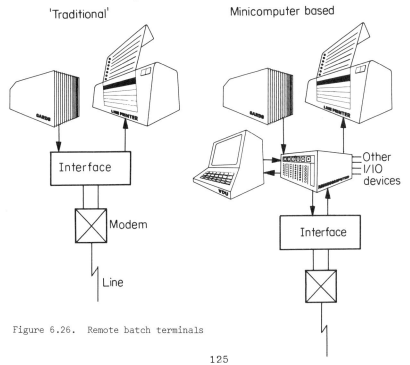

Figure 6.26. Remote batch terminals

A number of independent suppliers saw the mainframe manufacturers building up a substantial customer base using these devices. They considered that the peripherals used were available for use on minicomputers at a much lower cost and that minis themselves would prove to be very effective and flexible controllers. In order to make their 'alternative' product even more attractive, the miniprocessors were programmed to emulate the mainframe companies standard products, thus obviating the need to do any special programming at the central site. Such remote batch emulators have been produced for the ICL 7020, IBM 2780, Univac's DCT2000 and CDC's 200 User Terminal.

Other advantages of the minibased batch terminal are:

1. A wider range of peripherals is available (e.g. graph plotters, disc store).

2. Interactive terminals can be attached to the remote batch device.

3. Input can be pre-edited prior to transmission.

4. Data compression techniques can be applied to eliminate multiple blanks (and other characters) in card and print data. As the line speed is almost always the limiting factor, such techniques can often improve throughput by as much as 50% even where the peripherals operate at the same nominal speed.

5. Emulator packages can be changed so that the same terminal can be linked to different mainframes according to application needs.

6. Low cost.

Although IBM have recently tried to counter this market trend by introducing a cheaper terminal with hard-ware data compression capability, an increasing number of users tend to favour the intelligent device.

Another development that is becoming of increasing importance is the tendency to provide all small scale general purpose computers with communications adapters so that their local capabilities can be enhanced by the ability to link up to a large scale machine when extra power or storage is needed. This approach is relevant to the large corporate group of companies sharing large scale central site machines but also to small firms who are getting into computers for the first time. Such concerns can do small jobs and editing runs locally and then link up to a bureau computer, perhaps one offering a specialist service, as and when needed.

In conclusion it might be useful to differentiate between the two much abused terms: *Remote Batch Entry* and *Remote Job Entry* (Figure 6.27). The former, RBE, is applicable where the terminals are merely being used as remote peripherals to a central machine. Control is in the hands of the CPU operator who decides which jobs are going to be run and when, and tells the terminal operator which data cards to put in the reader or which stationery to load on the printer. In contrast, the RJE system gives control to the remote batch terminal operators and they decide which jobs they want to run and submit the appropriate control cards as well as the data; quite a different approach.

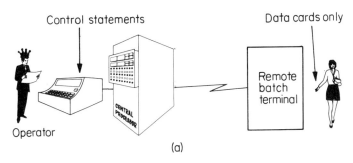

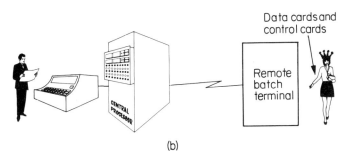

Figure 6.27. Comparison of (a) remote job and (b) remote batch entry

6.7 SPECIAL PURPOSE TERMINALS

The design of online systems has much to do with finding terminals which most suit particular application requirements. For reasons of economy and flexibility most designers try to use general purpose equipment where the application does not have to be 'distorted' too much in order to make it 'fit' the best available device. However, in some areas the potential market is big enough for suppliers to justify the production of a special purpose unit which, if not less expensive, then has more facilities of the right kind. It is not intended to describe here all the special purpose units that might be available but merely to give an indication of what is on the market. If the reader has a particular interest then he is advised to get in touch with suppliers directly.

Factory data collection

Some of the earliest special purpose devices were devised for the collection of data from the shop floor for production and inventory control purposes. The variables needed for this purpose tend to be as follows:

1. Time an event occurs (e.g. completion of a job).
2. Identification of a piece of work (a component moving through the factory).
3. Identification of the work station.
4. Identification of the work carried out.
5. Identification of the operative.
6. Identification of any parts used.
7. Details of rejects, exceptional conditions, etc.

Most, if not all, of the above data can be coded in numerics and entered by use of switch settings, prepunched cards (perhaps attached to items of work-in-progress), badges and so on.

The terminal should be simple to operate, rugged in construction (perhaps able to resist the occasional nudge from a forklift truck ...), properly shielded from electrical interference and insulated from other environmental influences such as dirt, vibration and so on. Such systems are linked by cables within a plant to a local controller which might produce cards, paper tape or magnetic tape offline for batch processing by the computer. Many systems now put the controllers directly online so that feedback is in the form of reports to line supervisors and management.

Bank teller machines.

Although a number of special terminals have been designed for banking (mostly as modifications to general purpose terminals) they tend to vary somewhat in view of the widely differing structures of the banking business from country to country. The primary problem for most banks (especially savings banks) is the maintenance of customers' passbooks. The online update of both passbooks and the customer's account within the computer, simultaneously, is by now a well established technique. Of course, once a terminal is installed it may also be used for enquiry purposes - very useful in terms of customer service.

Most of the U.K. Trustee Savings Banks have formed themselves into consortia in order to share computer facilities for such teleprocessing systems. To the present date the audit and other requirements of banks have been such that banking terminals are almost exclusively hard-copy. Some banking terminals have been designed with other objectives. IBM for example, produced a concentrator system which was designed to minimise the enormous line rentals which could be incurred by the U.K. clearing banks with many hundreds of branches. Burroughs concentrated on providing very flexible intelligent terminals which could perform a lot of banking functions within the branch. In 1973, IBM announced a new banking terminal system which although still concentrator based had a wider range of terminal devices including a 'Self scan' keyboard display and an online 'cash dispenser' which can be installed for use by customers inside or outside the branch.

Point of sale terminals

A very large market for terminals is retail distribution, i.e. shops stores, supermarkets (and hypermarkets?). Such systems have been somewhat slow to get off the ground, but the terminals themselves show a fair amount of ingenuity in design. The point-of-sale terminal typically comprises:

Cash register
Printer for producing sales slips
Printer for recording sales
Display of the cash amount of each item being entered and the
  final total
Means of recording the stock items sold for control purposes
Credit card reader
Staff card reader (for commission purposes)
Security locks
Controller

The easy recording of stock movements has mainly been solved by the use of 'bar encoded' strips of paper which can be attached to the products in the store. As the items go past the checkout point, the strips are read by a 'wand' or 'light pen' (Figure 6.28) and recorded (usually) on cassette tape. (It must be mentioned that, at the time of writing, most systems were set up for stock recording only; the strips being attached to shelves.) At the end of the day the cassette can be transmitted to the central computer (perhaps via a Midnight Line - *see* Chapter 10) which will then automatically arrange for replenishments. The 'wand' system is flexible enough for use in reading staff badges and where appropriate a customer's 'account' card.

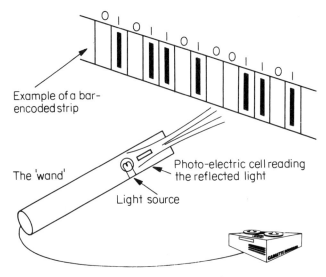

Example of a bar-encoded strip

The 'wand'

Photo-electric cell reading the reflected light

Light source

Figure 6.28.   Point of sale system: bar encoding

The U.K. firm Plessey have been very successful in implementing this type of equipment in libraries in the U.K. and Sweden.   Borrowers each have an ID card with an encoded strip and each book also has a strip inside the cover.   Simply by reading each of these, the librarian can quickly and easily record details of books taken on loan.

QUESTIONS, DISCUSSION TOPICS AND ASSIGNMENTS

1. Discuss the pros and cons of using special-purpose terminals wherever possible in preference to general-purpose devices.

2. Ignoring any economic considerations, what procedural benefits might there be in the use of interactive batch devices as an alternative to a remote batch terminal?   What disadvantages might there be?

3. Redraw and extend Figure 6.5 to show the sequence of events for a synchronous device.   Pay particular attention to the timing problems.

4. Under what circumstances would a front-feed forms shute be of use?

5. When might a whole character impact printer be preferable to a matrix mechanism (in spite of lower speed)?

6. When would you recommend the use of unbuffered keyboard printers on multipoint circuits?

7. Why might 'micro-programmed' logic be particularly relevant to data transmission terminals?

8. Obtain from IBM details of their 2760 microfilm terminal. Suggest five possible applications for it.

9. Discuss the relative merits of keyboard/printers and visual display units (both standalone and cluster).

10. For a particular manufacturer investigate the relative merits of standalone and cluster visual displays. Draw a breakeven chart for costs.

11. Take any form with which you are familiar and design a VDU screen layout using forms made in such a way that an operator could readily enter data directly from the original document. List the sequence of keys which the operator would need to press.

12. "There is little or no future for remote batch terminals because the cost of a number of interactive devices has dropped below the cost of an equivalent remote batch terminal and its associated data preparation units." Discuss.

13. Only three special-purpose terminals are described in Chapter 6. List five more such devices and describe two of them in detail.

IBM 3741 Data Stations are used to record data on 'Diskettes' (floppy discs). Periodically, the Diskettes can be collected from the data stations and transferred to a device which transmits the encoded information to the computer centre. A printer may be included in the configuration to receive reports from the centre. A programmable version of the data station was announced at the beginning of 1974. *Courtesy IBM United Kingdom Ltd.*

The ICL 7020 Remote Batch Terminal. This is a hard-wired device shown here with a card reader, line printer and control teletype. The controller is in the far corner. *Courtesy ICL.*

A Feedback OS 436 Terminal used for time and attendance recording.
Courtesy Feedback Data Ltd.

An IBM System 3 Model 10 small business computer. These machines have
become quite popular as powerful remote batch terminals. *Courtesy
IBM United Kingdom Ltd.*

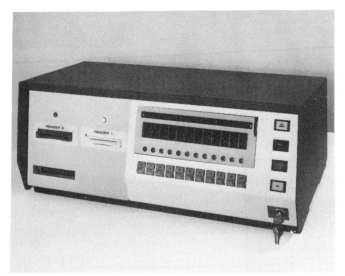

A more sophisticated terminal made by Feedback for shop-floor data
collection. This version can accept an 80 column punched card, a
plastic ID badge and a certain amount of hand input variable data.
A security lock can be seen at the bottom right of the unit. *Courtesy
Feedback Data Ltd.*

An online cash dispenser - the IBM 3614 can also accept requests for
cheque books and statements and a small display can be used for balance
enquiries. *Courtesy IBM United Kingdom Ltd.*

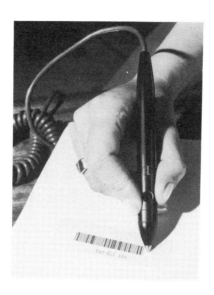

The Plessey light pen. See text for details. *Courtesy Plessey Co. Ltd.,*
Data Systems Unit.

The Racal-Milgo Ltd., MC 70 time division multiplexor. *Courtesy*
Racal-Milgo Ltd.

CHAPTER 7
MULTIPLEXORS AND CONCENTRATORS

The simplest way of connecting terminals to a central computer is on a straightforward point-to-point basis (Figure 7.1). The line rental for point-to-point networks can be very high and one technique that can be used to minimise this is to *share* lines (Figure 7.2). Chapter 4 described possible different ways of multidropping and Chapter 10 describes the techniques which are possible in the U.K. There are however, two other techniques which can be used to reduce line costs and they involve the use of:

Multiplexors

Concentrators

These two terms tend to be used interchangeably, but the units are quite different. If any one criteria can be applied to differentiate them it is that the multiplexor is *transparent* and the concentrator is not.

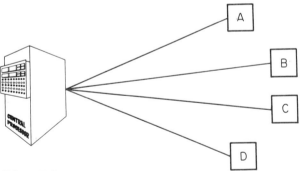

Figure 7.1.   Point-to-point network

7.1   MULTIPLEXORS

First of all the reader is advised to avoid the confusion of these

136

communications multiplexors with multiplexor I/0 channels on central
processors. Let us assume that Figure 7.1 shows four low speed terminals
working at 300 bits/sec and all sited close together but at some distance
from the computer. To adopt the multidrop solution (Figure 7.2) would

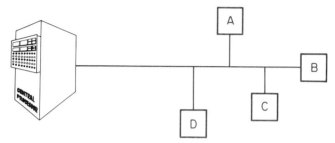

Figure 7.2. Multidropped network

require that the terminals be addressable and, possibly, buffered. An
alternative approach not requiring any change in the terminals and their
method of operation would be the use of multiplexors as shown in Figure
7.3. Clearly, the data from the four terminals is now passing down one
telephone line covering the long distance between the area of the terminals
and the computer centre. How is this done without affecting the terminals?
The approach is to 'channelise' the main circuit providing one sub-channel
for each terminal using one of two possible techniques:

    Frequency division multiplexing (FDM) or

    Time division multiplexing (TDM)

(The lines between the terminals and the remote multiplexor may be leased
private circuits or dialled on the PSN.)

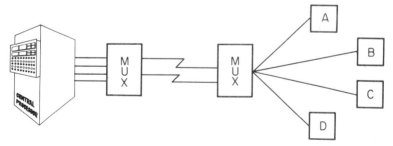

Figure 7.3. Multiplexor network

7.2 FREQUENCY DIVISION MULTIPLEXING

Chapter 4 described various techniques for sub-channelling lines to obtain full duplex working (Figures 4.25 and 4.26). FDM extends the idea of having multiple carriers from two only up to one per attached terminal in each direction. Four wire medium speed circuits are used, one pair in each direction in order to continue the FDX working right from the terminals through the multiplexed line. Each pair is then channelised so that each terminal has its own mark and space frequencies (Figure 7.4). The number of terminals that might be attached will be a function of:

The speed of the low speed lines
The speed of the medium speed lines
The number of medium speed lines

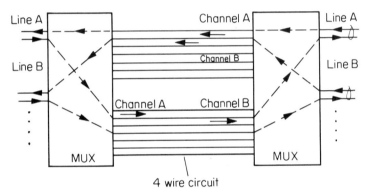

Figure 7.4.   Frequency division multiplexing

As an example, the U.K. Post Office Dataplex 1 service will handle:

Six 110 bits/sec terminals on a 1200 baud circuit
Twelve 110 bits/sec terminals on a 2400 baud circuit

FDM multiplexors are normally hardware units and are very limited in terms of the number of terminals that can be attached and the mixture of line codes used by the terminals. The Dataplex 1 mentioned above is designed for standard 10 ch/sec ASCII Teletypes.

7.3 TIME DIVISION MULTIPLEXING

The majority of multiplexors presently on the market use the TDM technique. No sub-channelling of the main circuit is used and data

is passed between the multiplexors by the regular two way exchange of
blocks. (Figure 7.5). Each terminal is allocated a specific character
position within each block. If the operator of terminal C, for example,
presses key 'L' the letter 'L' is inserted in the third position of the
next block to be transmitted. Similarly, characters being sent from the
computer to terminal C will be carried in position 3 of the blocks being
received by the remote multiplexor. As with FDM it is normal to use one
or more 4-wire medium speed circuits (1200 to 9600 bits/sec) between the
multiplexors. Each pair is used for transmission in one direction only.
Supervisory channels might be used for acknowledging the receipt of a
good block.

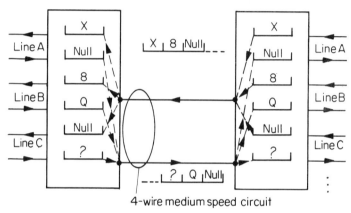

Figure 7.5.   Time division multiplexing

Many TDM multiplexors are programmable devices. They are microprogrammed
(firmware) devices at the lower end of the scale, and based upon fully
programmable minis at the top end. This flexibility enables a wider range
of line speeds and codes to be attached without expensive hardware modifications. The software in the multiplexor scans low speed line buffers
for completed characters at fixed time intervals. Where a character is
ready it is moved to the output block. Otherwise a null character is
inserted in the equivalent position. At the end of the cycle the block
is transmitted on the medium speed circuit and the scan of the low speed
lines continues. Simultaneously with this, the characters (including
nulls) to the low speed output buffers and transmits them to the terminals.

An example of capacities possible on a hardware device is provided by
the CODEX 810 which can multiplex onto one 9600 bits/sec circuit:

4 lines at 1200 bits/sec

139

8 lines at 150 bits/sec

Various codes can be accommodated.

The Texas Instruments 960A minicomputer can be used as a multiplexor to handle up to 256 110 bits/sec lines on three 9600 bits/sec main circuits. The number of lines at other speeds can be handled on a pro-rata basis.

7.4 MULTIPLEXOR ARRANGEMENTS

There are various line arrangements possible with multiplexors, part-icularly with respect to modems. Figure 7.6 illustrates alternative ways in which both FDM and TDM multiplexors can be installed. TDM units can also be multidropped and Figure 7.7 shows a technique used in the Racal Milgo T-20 whereby each multiplexor passes blocks on down the circuit until they reach the relevant device.

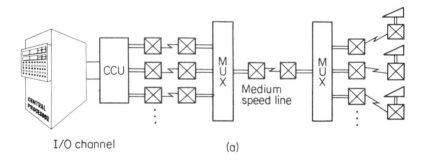

I/O channel   (a)

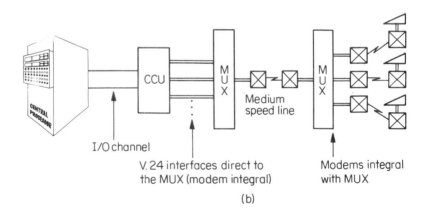

I/O channel

V. 24 interfaces direct to   Modems integral
the MUX (modem integral)   with MUX

(b)

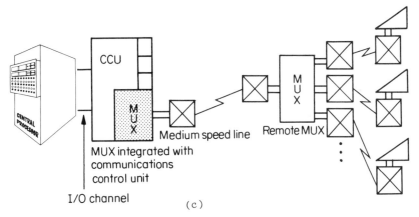

CCU

MUX

Medium speed line   Remote MUX

MUX integrated with
communications
control unit

I/O channel   (c)

Figure 7.6.   Alternative multiplexor arrangements

    (a) Modems used throughout the system

    (b) Modems integrated with the multiplexors

    (c) Multiplexor integral with the communications
          control unit

It must be remembered that, whatever arrangement or technique used,
the multiplexors should be transparent to both the CPU software and the
terminal operator. In other words it should not be possible for either
to distinguish between working directly on a point-to-point line or
through a multiplexor.

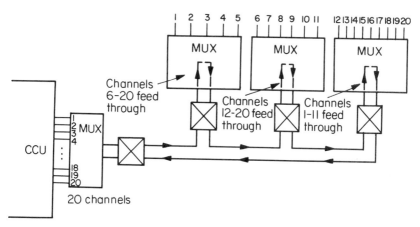

Figure 7.7.   Technique for multidropping multiplexors (Racal Milgo T-20)

141

7.5   CONCENTRATORS

Concentrators are fundamentally different from multiplexors in the following ways:

1. Concentrators are not transparent and can be addressed from the computer as though they were terminals. The terminals attached to the concentrators would have sub-addresses.
2. Concentrators work on a block-by-block basis and not character-by-character as in a multiplexor.
3. Concentrators are always programmable and could have peripherals.
4. A 'mirror image' device is not required at the central site and data can be 'deconcentrated' in the CPU software, thus minimising hardware costs.

Concentrators then are a means of minimising line rentals (Figure 7.8) but can also be a means of distributing intelligence from the central computer. This latter can often be an economical alternative in some systems to having intelligent terminals.

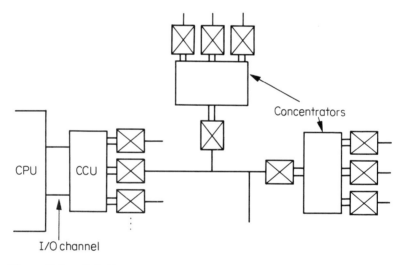

Figure 7.8.   Multidropped concentrators

The terminals used in such systems are often low speed 'idiot' devices but this need not be the case. Also, they are normally attached on point-to-point circuits (which may be leased or dialled) but there is no reason why multidropping should not be used where appropriate. It should be noted however that this would certainly increase the complexity

142

of the software in the concentrator. The concentrators themselves could be multidropped but in the situation where each one has large numbers of terminals attached, care should be taken to ensure that the main circuit is of adequate speed. The main functions of the concentrator (Figure 7.9) are usually:

1. To receive data from the terminals.
2. To carry out any vetting required.
3. To attach the appropriate sub-address to each incoming message and to place it in the main output buffer.
4. When the main output buffer is full, transmit the data to the CPU when a polling sequence is received.
5. To respond to selective as well as generalised polling (*see* Chapter 5 on polling).

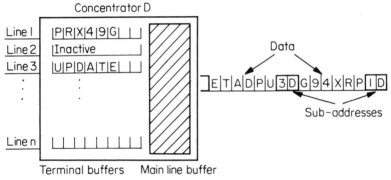

Figure 7.9.   Concentrator buffering and data formats

As concentrators are usually based upon standard product minicomputers, it is possible to put peripherals on them. This may be necessary anyway for program loading. Low capacity fixed or exchangeable discs could be used to hold files for many purposes:

1. Reference files for data vetting and manipulation (e.g. product codes, price lists).
2. To hold input screen layouts where the terminals are VDUs.
3. To hold input data when the main circuit has failed, thus enabling data input to continue.

(*See* Chapter 9 for more detailed discussion of minicomputers.)

On systems where the availability of the network is important, it may be desirable to interconnect the concentrators such that each one always has an alternative main circuit and is capable of accepting data on it for onward transmission on behalf of another concentrator (Figure 7.10).

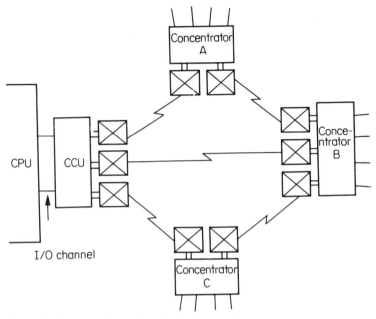

Figure 7.10. Network of interlinked concentrators

QUESTIONS, DISCUSSION TOPICS AND ASSIGNMENTS

1. Discuss the techniques of multidropping and remote multiplexing. Where would one approach be used in preference to the other?

2. Why are minicomputers often used as time division multiplexors? (You may prefer to read Chapter 9 before answering this question.)

3. One side advantage of programmable concentrators is that they put computing power into the network. Describe some of the ways in which this power could be used.

CHAPTER 8

CONTROL UNITS AND FRONT-END PROCESSORS

In the last few chapters, the various components which can be used
to establish a data communications network; terminals, modems, concentrators and multiplexors, have been described. We now move right into
the centre of the system and look at the equipment needed in the computer
room itself. The incoming telephone lines will, of course, terminate
at the modems,. What do we need to put between the computer's input/output
channel and the modem interface cables so that we can write programs which
will send data to and receive data from the terminals? The device used
is the *Communications Control Unit* (CCU). This term covers a device
which is implemented in a wide variety of forms.

8.1   COMMUNICATIONS CONTROL UNIT

The CCU needs to be able to carry out:

1. Parallel-to-serial and serial-to-parallel conversion of
    bits within a character.

2. Framing of characters with start-stop bits for asynchronous
    communications.

3. Insertion and deletion of synchronising characters in
    synchronous communications (on some CCUs).

4. Identifying control characters.

5. Error detection through the use of character and block
    parity checking.

6. Where necessary, automatic dialling and automatic answering
    of calls on the public telephone network.

7. Interface with the communications lines via modems or line
    adapters.

8. Interface with the main processor input/output channel.

9. Automatic polling (on some CCU's only).

145

In its simplest form, CCUs on minis are single-line interfaces each with a different address on the I/O bus (Figure 8.1).

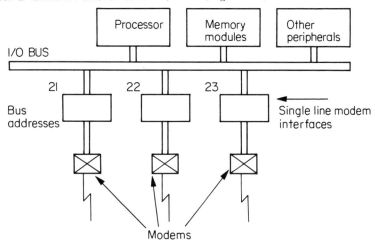

Figure 8.1.   Single line modem interfaces on a minicomputer

These self-contained modem interfaces can be quite economical where only a few lines need to be attached. They are available for start-stop and synchronous working. However, as the number of lines increases the benefits from sharing the circuitry to perform some of the above functions becomes accordingly greater. Still talking in terms of minicomputers, the arrangement in Figure 8.2 can work in one of two different ways:

Bit multiplexing

Character multiplexing

Bit multiplexing is very simple and inexpensive; each line is sampled for bits on a cyclic basis and the bits obtained are passed straight through to storage for assembly as characters. Such an arrangement is low cost and very suitable for slower speed lines. But the technique imposes a big overhead on the system because memory cycles are being stolen at least 8 or 9 times per character. So, as the number and speed of lines increase, the system overhead becomes more unacceptable and leaves less time for actually processing the data. The solution adopted is to put character buffers in the interface (*see* Figure 6.5). This means that the processor is only interrupted for each character rather than each bit. On synchronous adapters the buffer will often be able to take two characters to assist in identifying pairs of SYN characters (which can then be rejected). The 'stand-alone' modem adapters described earlier

146

are almost always buffered.

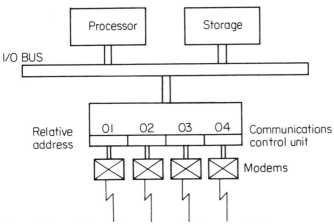

Figure 8.2.   Minicomputer communications controller

The 'traditional' approach with general purpose machines is very similar

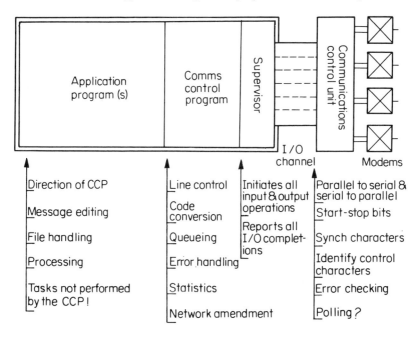

Figure 8.3.   Central site configuration using a hardware CCU

147

(Figure 8.3). Each line (not terminal) on the control unit has a separate channel address like a tape unit or card reader. As with most computer control units these CCUs are completely hard-wired and this has proved to be embarrassing to both suppliers and customers alike. The range of combinations of line speed, codes and transmission techniques imposes considerable problems for manufacturers in the design and configuration of such hardware CCUs. The problem for the user has been that of costs. The solution which has developed has been that of the *front-end processor*.

8.2   FRONT-END PROCESSORS

The initial development of the 'front-end' parallels that of the minicomputer based remote batch terminal. Mini-processor manufacturers (and some users) identified a situation where standard hardware controllers could be replaced by a small scale processor at significantly lower cost and with clear advantages in terms of flexibility. Figure 8.4 shows a possible revised allocation of tasks between the various units concerned.

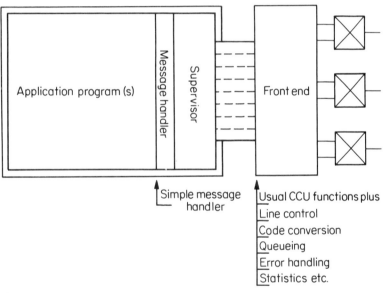

Figure 8.4   Central site configuration using a front-end processor

But before one can assess the benefits of front ending, it is important to determine what communications functions are performed by the central processor. Figure 8.3 shows the three main software components of an online system. Each is described in more detail below.

148

The supervisor

This is the standard operating system control program for the computer being used. This might be ICL George 3, Burroughs MCP, IBM MFTII, etc. (Some supervisors need to be generated with special facilities when data communications are to be used.) Apart from data and job management, it is the function of the supervisor to initiate and monitor all I/O operations and this effectively means that it controls the I/O channel.

The communications control program (CCP)

This is software supplied by the computer manufacturer in order to provide the customer with certain facilities, some of which are essential to the operation of a data communications network and others intended to ease the task of the application program in administering the terminals. Most CCPs provide the facilities described below.

Line control (sometimes called 'line protocol'). This involves the periodic 'polling' of terminals to see if they wish to transmit data of 'addressing' ('selecting') to determine whether a particular terminal is able to receive data (*see* Chapter 5). Some CCUs (the IBM 2703 for example) are able to carry out polling sequences automatically and only interrupt the main processor on finding a terminal which wishes to transmit data.

Code conversion. A line 'code' is the convention determining the pattern of bits used to represent characters of information on communications circuits, (*see* Chapter 5). Quite often these codes do not correspond to the convention used within the computer. It is necessary, therefore, for incoming messages to be translated from the line code to main processor code and vice versa for outgoing data. When one considers that, despite efforts to standardise, codes also differ from terminal to terminal, translation can be a significant operation in terms of time and storage.

Buffering and queueing. It is common in a communications system for a situation to arise where messages are arriving from terminals faster than the central processor can deal with them. Under these circumstances, a queue forms until the backlog is cleared. The administration of such queues in core storage (and sometimes on disc) is a job carried out to varying degrees of sophistication by the CCP available.

Error handling and recovery. When an error condition of some kind is reported by the CCU, the control program has to decide on and initiate remedial action. Lower forms of CCP have only rudimentary error handling

149

and many conditions must be referred to the application program.

Collation and analysis of statistics. This continuing job is carried out for the purpose of detecting possible line degradation and providing details of equipment loading for network administration purposes.

Amendment of network. It is sometimes necessary for the system to stop using certain lines and start using others. The CCP provides facilities for this to be done, but under the direction of the user program.

The application program (AP)

This is that part of the system designed and written by the user to fulfill his particular needs. In general, the following tasks are performed; the initiation and control of those functions performed by the CCP; the execution of those network control functions *not* performed by the CCP available; the vetting of incoming messages (equivalent to the edit programs in a batch environment); the processing of incoming messages and, where applicable, the transmission of outgoing messages; and the collation and summary of statistics not provided by the CCP.

It will now be evident to many programmers, that a CCP for even a moderately sized data communications system would require a substantial amount of main storage. Thirty to 100K bytes (in addition to a similar quantity for the supervisor) would not be abnormal. CCUs tend to be more expensive than control units for in-house peripherals and one would expect to pay £20,000 to £60,000 for a CCU to handle more than 15 medium speed or more than 50 low speed lines. This cost may need to be doubled if a stand-by system is required. On second generation computers, standard CCUs (or any interface with telecommunications) were few indeed. Much data communications pioneering work was done with one-off 'lash-up' CCUs often interfacing to the central processor as tape units. Today, all manufacturers of both large and small computers provided such equipment. With a few exceptions these CCUs are solid electronics and therefore tend to be inflexible in their ability to cope with the wide variety of terminals available. A few manufacturers have minimised this problem by making their CCU programmable (*see* Figure 8.4). The Honeywell Datanet 30 and the Burroughs Data Communications Processor are both examples of this approach. As software is more flexible than hardware, this solution offers obvious advantages. But the use of such 'front-end processors' offers less obvious benefits in easing the main processor of much of the CCP burden. This point is worthy of further examination.

Referring to the earlier summary of control program functions, a programmable CCU of only modest capability should be able to undertake

150

the following:

Line control. The CCU would be able to relieve the main processor of the chore of polling apparently inactive terminals to locate one ready to transmit. Such an automatic operation may be extended to include facilities for transmission to single terminals or broadcasting to groups.

Code conversion. The CCU could hold translation tables for all the codes being used in the network. Thus the main processor need only consider data in its own internal format.

Buffering and queueing. Instead of passing single characters on to the main processor, the CCU could assemble whole messages and form these into queues.

Error handling and recovery. A programmable CCU would not only be able to detect errors but, in many instances, be able to activate resends without CCP or application program intervention.

Collation and analysis of statistics. This is another routine but an important job which could be undertaken by the control unit.

Amendment of network. As well as enabling and disabling lines at application program request, a programmable CCU could itself decide such action. Where important lines are duplicated for safety purposes, switchover could be automatic.

In addition to the above, there is no reason why the CCU should not perform some editing and vetting of incoming data. Even sophisticated terminals such as the Burroughs TC 500 transmit data in free format for optimum line utilisation. A significant proportion of main processor time is taken by manipulating such data into a more easily handled form. In addition to doing this, the control unit could verify syntax, requesting resend where necessary, with AP intervention. Because standard range minicomputers are often used for front ending it is possible to attach peripherals. This facilitates the writing of network activity logs or backup files onto tape as a CCU activity. Similarly a disc store could be used to hold high level database indices for attachment to enquiry or update messages on their way through to the CCPU. This overlap can be very beneficial when using high capacity moving head disc on the processor. The front-ends described above attach directly to the CPU's I/O channel and, usually, have a single address rather than one per line. It may be worth mentioning that some early front-ends interfaced to the CPU through an intermediate disc store, provided 'inbuilt' queueing and enabled the processor to work in batch mode (Figure 8.5).

151

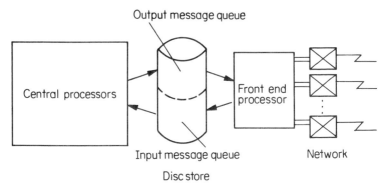

Figure 8.5.   Front-end processor using an intermediate disc store

8.3   A NEW BREED OF COMMUNICATIONS DEVICE

Over the past few years front ending has become 'respectable'! IBM,
ICL and UNIVAC have all announced communications controllers which can
be used both as a front-end and as a remote concentrator. In the case
of ICL and UNIVAC the controllers are available for attachment to any
manufacturers CPU.

The development which has made this change possible is the concept
of the 'soft line interface'. In the past, interfaced had to be
engineered for specific line requirements. Now it is possible to
obtain an interface which acts as a peripheral to the processor in the
CCU (or concentrator) and has registers which can be loaded with the
values needed to make it handle any type of circuit. The register will
hold the following variables:

    Asynchronous or Synchronous working
    Number of bits per character
    Number of stop bits
    Speed of line
    Value of SYN characters
    Odd or even parity.

As minis are quite difficult to program, manufacturers are supplying
high level languages for user development purposes. NCP from IBM and
CORAL from ICL. (Figure 8.6 shows the different ways in which such
general purpose communications controllers can be used in a network.)
Chapter 9 goes into more detail about minicomputer systems.

152

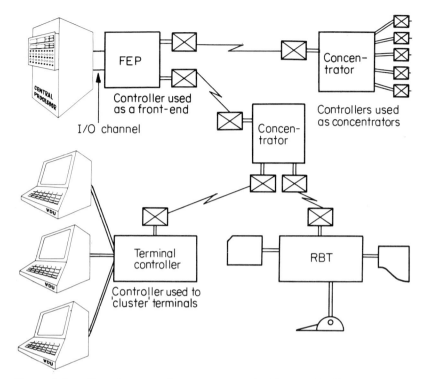

Figure 8.6.   Uses for general purpose communications controller

QUESTIONS, DISCUSSION TOPICS AND ASSIGNMENTS

1. What criteria would you use to distinguish between a programmable
   CCU and a front-end processor?   Is the difference of any relevance?

2. Investigate the hardware and software used in a fairly typical
   mini-computer system (e.g. a DEC PDP-11/40) and analyse it according
   to the various functions listed in Chapter 8.

3. Repeat question 2 but for a general purpose computer such as an
   ICL 1900 or a Univac 9000 series.

4. Obtain details of the Honeywell Datanet 200, IBM 3705 and ICL 7905,
   and draw up a comparison matrix of facilities.

CHAPTER 9
THE MINICOMPUTER IN DATA COMMUNICATIONS

One of the few sectors of the data processing business to rival teleprocessing in terms of growth is that of minicomputers. This chapter discusses some of the implications of using minicomputers in data communications systems; as terminal, concentrators, multiplexors, front-ends and even central processors. The role that minicomputers are now playing in teleprocessing is so important that this book would not be complete without an evaluation of that role.

9.1 OVERVIEW

The use of the term 'minicomputer' has come to mean much more than just 'small computer', although many still use the word in this way. Before listing the main characteristics of these machines, it should be pointed out that small-scale general-purpose systems such as IBM System 3, 360 Model 20, ICL 1901A and Burroughs B500 have been excluded. Although all these devices can be used as intelligent terminals, they do not fall within the classification of minis, and have been put in the total context of communications hardware at a later point. Particular attention is paid to minis because they are playing and will continue to play a special role in the development of teleprocessing systems. This section, then, discusses the main characteristics of the following aspects of minis; hardware, software, firmware (or microprogramming) and communications. (This broad view is being taken because many of the commercially orientated readers of this book will have had little experience of minis.)

Incidentally, the terms 'micro' and 'midi' are becoming as popular as 'mini'. They do not loom large in the vocabulary of this book, but where they are used assume no more than: micro computer equals small mini; and midi computer equals big mini.

Table 9.1   *Hardware characteristics of minicomputer processors*

Characteristics	Availability		
	Minimum	Typical	Maximum
Memory			
Word length, data bits	8	12 or 16	24
Size, words	1k	4-32k	128k
Cycle time, μsec	8	1	0·5
Memory parity	No	Optional	Standard
Memory protect	No	Optional	Standard
Direct addressing, page size	256	4096	All of core
Indirect addressing	No	Yes	Multilevel
Processor			
Instruction set	8	20-50	Over 100
General-purpose registers	1	4-16	128
Index registers	None	1-4	15
Hardware multiply/divide	No	Optional	Standard
Immediate instructions	No	Sometimes	Yes
Double-word instructions	No	Sometimes	Yes
Byte processing	No	Sometimes	Yes
Input/output			
Programmed I/O channel	1	1	1
I/O word size, bits	8	8-18	18
Priority interrupts	1	1-16	Up to 256
Direct memory access	No	Optional	Optional
I/O maximum transfer rate, kHz	125,000	200,000 to 600,000	1,000,000
Other features			
Real-time clock	No	Optional	Standard
Power fail/restart	Optional	Standard	Standard
Exchangeable disc, Mch	No	1M to 10M	200M
Purchase price			
Processor with display panel, 8k words and teletype	£2,000	£4,000	£8,000

9.2   MINI HARDWARE

Table 9.1 and 9.2 list the hardware and software characteristics of minicomputers presently available. From the view-point of a programmer used to writing software for 360/370, 1900 and so on, what are the major features of a typical mini? Let us take as an example a recently announced computer which a typical middle-of-the-road mini, and see how it fits in with the total picture drawn by the tables. For convenience call it the

Tiny 16. At first glance the performance of the system seems incredible; a 1 μsec cycle-time - half that of the 360 Model 50. A good motor cycle may travel faster than an Inter-City express, but to choose speed as the sole measure of power is obviously absurd. It is equally absurd to do so when comparing the power of computers. The difference is that a lot of pencil-power is required to program a Tiny 16 to match the over-all capability of a Model 50. The Tiny has a 33-command instruction set compared with the 50's which is in the region of 140. An example of the effect of this difference is the storage-to-storage move. A single MVC instruction on the 360 would take 110·69 μsec to move 100 bytes, whereas the Tiny would need to perform 50 register loads and stores taking 545 μsec (including the overhead involved in controlling the loop), and about twice as much memory space. As its name implies, the Tiny 16 has a 16-bit word memory (as against 24-bit in the 1900 and 32-bit in the 360/370 ranges) which is available in 4k increments up to a maximum of 64k. Each 4k 'page' is directly addressable by instructions located within that page. If you wish to refer to data outside a block, indirect addressing commands must be used. Data is transferred to and from low-speed peripherals on a word-by-word basis, the program having to handle each individual character. Fast peripherals such as tape and disc are attached via a direct memory access feature which enables whole messages to be transferred, the program being interrupted only on completion.

Table 9.2 *Software characteristics of minicomputers*

| Characteristics | Availability | | |
	Minimum	Typical	Maximum
Assembler	Yes	Yes (including interactive)	Yes (including interactive)
Macro language	No	Sometimes	Yes
Compiler	No	BASIC FORTRAN	FORTRAN IV (perhaps interactive) ALGOL sometimes COBOL and CORAL
Job sequencer	No	Yes	Yes
Library facilities	No	Sometimes	Yes
Operating system	No	Sometimes RTOS	Real-time dual Programming
File handling	No	Sometimes	Yes

Other hardware features available include memory-protect, a real-time clock, multilevel priority interrupt and floating point arithmetic. The range of peripherals is, as you would expect, less than that offered by the big mainframe companies, but it does cover cards, paper tape, line printers and magnetic tape and exchangeable disc as well as graph plotters, digital/analogue subsystems and communications multiplexors (of which, more later).

9.3 MINI SOFTWARE

On the software side, Tiny Computers Limited offer an assembler which has a useful little 'linkage editor' and a macro generator, which is really essential for minis. At a higher level there is a single-pass FORTRAN II compiler and a conversational program for mathematical calculations. Of increasing importance are Operating Systems and the Tiny has TOS-16 which supports dual programming, storage protect, file handling for disc and   tape, program loading, debugging and so on. In addition there are about 10 utility programs.

9.4 FIRMWARE

The 'heart' of some minis is an ultra-fast microprocessor (cycle-time less than 100 nsec) with an instruction set of perhaps 5 or 6 commands which is 'programmed' to interpret and execute the main system commands. This 'programming' or micro 'programming' is usually performed at the manufacturing stage by automatically or semi-automatically wiring fast read-only memories (ROMs). However, with some systems this wiring or circuitry can be modified in the field. It is this flexible technique of 'making the commands work' (rather than using solid electronics) that enables some minis to have extensive instruction sets including specialist operations in areas such as list processing, analogue interfacing and data communications. Indeed, many systems are completely transparent, which is why the technique has become popular with large scale machines; 370s can look like 1900s, B1700s can look like anything you care to name... The technique is particularly relevant to repetitive operations and data communications has a lot of these, e.g. assembling bits from lines, performing parity checks and so on.

9.5 COMMUNICATIONS

Minicomputers are ideally suited to dedicated communications tasks, their speed, low-cost core, expansibility and flexibility make them excellent machines for use in teleprocessing. They are compact, reliable,

will work from a 13A ring main - all of which are important factors when
equipment is to be installed in user offices. The cost of line multiplexors
for minis is very low. The Tiny 16, for example, has a 16-line multiplexor
base costing less than £1,000 to which has to be added an adapter £200-£400
for each line. The whole of this area will be discussed in more depth later.

9.6   CURRENT USAGE

The terminology and concepts of minicomputers have been summarised
and now the current practice of using programmable devices in general,
and minis in particular, in remote terminal systems will be described.

9.7   TERMINALS

Probably the first successful, purpose-built 'intelligent' terminal
was the Burroughs TC 500, initially marketed to the U.K. clearing banks.

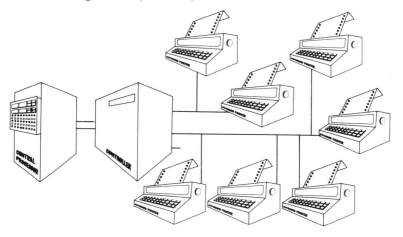

Figure 9.1.   Multidropped programmable terminals

This produced configurations as shown in Figure 9.1. The terminals are
fully programmable computers in their own right (although not really minis)
and use an inbuilt fixed-head disc as main memory. They were capable of:
editing input transactions (including check-digit verification and batch
total checking); the batching of data prior to transmission; the priority
channelling of enquiries; the acceptance and holding of output data prior
to printing; the formatting of input and output messages; the operation
of 'peripherals' such as paper tape, cassettes, etc. And this list
indicates the tasks normally required of intelligent terminals. The TC500
has a good assembler which can be used on the terminal itself and now also

158

a COBOL compiler. It is interesting that the terminal uses a firmware concept which is based upon micro-programs stored on read-only sections of the disc memory. A comparable device from Nixdorf is the 820/03. This terminal is preprogrammed by the supplier and the ROM is wired at the plant.

The increasingly popular VDU is now available in intelligent form and the Incoterm and Datapoint 2200 have integral minicomputers. The other main class of terminal in use is the remote batch entry device such as the ICL 7020, IBM 2780 and Univac DCT-2000. Intelligent RBTs such as the IBM 1130, 360 Model 20 and the UCC Cope Series have been with us for some time, and although some mainframe manufacturers continue to produce 'idiot' terminals, the trend is towards using existing small computers such as the 2901, System/3, 9200 and so on. At the less 'respectable' end of the market a number of independent companies successfully attacked IBM's large 2780 market by producing plug-for-plug compatible mini-based systems. These included Data 100 Model 78 and EAL's DCT-132.

9.8 MULTIPLEXORS AND CONCENTRATORS

IBM's solution to the U.K. Banks' teleprocessing needs was the 3980 concentrator system which is illustrated in Figure 9.2. The software in the 3891 concentrator (an IBM 1130) is quite different from that in the TC500. Because it is necessary for all the keyboard/printer terminals to operate simultaneously, the software has to be serially re-entrant with event and data tables for each terminal. User programs are pre-compiled on a System/360 and then merged into the supervisor software on an 1130 which produces an 'object' paper tape for loading into the 3981.

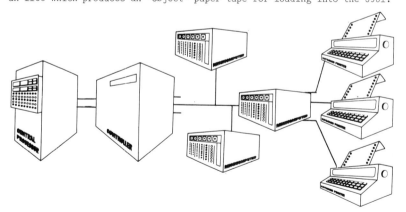

Figure 9.2. Multidropped programmable concentrators

Strictly speaking, no object program is produced; the concentrator operating system interprets a table of commands produced by the compiler from the source program. The language is well designed for commercial use. Sub-routines for different message types are activated by pressing special function keys and message formatting, CDV, priority enquiries, blocking and batch totalling are fully supported.

9.9   FRONT-END PROCESSING

The technique of 'front-end processing' has been with us in a number of forms for some time (Figure 9.3). Univac, Honeywell, Burroughs, recently ICL and (in the U.S.A.) IBM, have all used pre-processors. Minicomputer suppliers such as DEC and Interdata have front-ends available for many large-scale mainframes. Essentially, the hardware CCU is replaced by a programmable system giving greater flexibility in the choice of terminals used. In addition the FEP is usually able to take over many of the control programs and even a few of the application programs. As yet no special programming languages have been developed for front-ends and programming them can be one of the most difficult tasks in the data communications field.

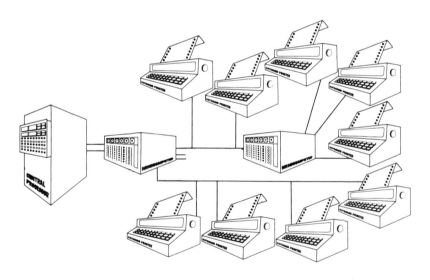

Figure 9.3.   Front-end processing (with other intelligent devices in network)

9.10   CENTRAL PROCESSOR

Systems designers are increasingly identifying application areas where minicomputers (normally a 'grid' of 2 or more) are more suitable than general purpose processors. These applications usually have certain things in common:

1. They are communications oriented.
2. They typically perform one application only.
3. The processor is more concerned with the storage and handling of data rather than computing it.

Figure 9.4 shows a pair of minicomputers used in an information retrieval application. The datafiles are generated by a general-purpose computer overnight, and passed to the mini system via paper tape at the beginning of each day.

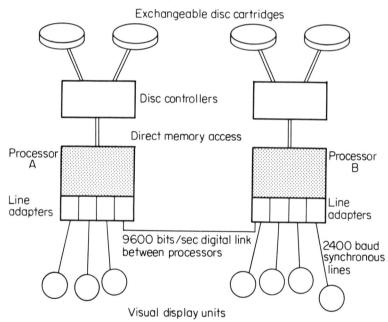

Figure 9.4.   Minicomputers used as a central processor in a communications system

9.11   THE FUTURE

Tasks which need to be performed at each level in the network have been indicated in previous chapters and in Figure 8.3. The standard of software available at each of the levels to assist the programmer has been discussed by splitting into communications control software and special-purpose compilers (or at least existing compilers suitably adapted), and the minis have been shown separately from other types of systems. (Table 9.3).

Table 9.3 *Standards of communications-oriented software*

Central processors	*Mini-based*	*Large-scale GP*
Compilers	Fair	Generally good
CCPs	Poor	Excellent
Front-ends	Mini-based	Special-purpose
Compilers	Coral only	Improving
CCPs	Fair	Not known
Concentrators	Mini-based	Special-purpose
Compilers	Coral only	Good
CCPs	Fair	Fair
Terminals	Mini-based	Others
Compilers	Non-existent	Good
CCPs	Poor	Good

At CPU level communications software is now very good, especially those packages incorporating file-handling facilities. Similarly, compilers have improved but sometimes one still ends up analysing bit indicators in COBOL. Outside the CPU the picture is very grim.. The TC500 has a form of COBOL and the System/3 has communications facilities in its RPGII compiler, but neither of these could be described as languages designed for, or suitable for the interactive checking and transmission of data on terminals. The IBM 3981 compiler is an excellent example of how such specialist software can be produced, but for marketing reasons this device is not available outside the banking industry.

Software requirements

Individual mainframe manufacturers will produce special languages for use with particular purpose-built terminals as IBM have done with their 3735. However, these devices tend to be very expensive compared with many mini-based configurations. Notwithstanding the fact that the

162

flexible nature of today's hardware is producing increasingly complex
systems more precisely tailored to application needs, many aspects of
communications network logic are still common to all users. Some examples
are: the compression of data; the block fields; the expansion and
display of codes received from a keyboard; batch total checking; check-
digit verification.

In my opinion, for the larger minicomputer suppliers, it would be
worth investing in the development of higher-level programming languages
designed to perform some of the tasks. They have already done this with
real-time operating systems, i.e. the *control* functions, and it would
only be a logical extension of this policy to cover the applications
areas of data-vetting and message formatting. Such packages will certainly
attract many more companies to the use of these low-cost processors in
their networks; at present, programming costs are higher than they need
to be because of the difficulty of programming minis for this kind of work.

As computing power becomes cheaper and more compact, the need to communicate power is diminishing and the need to transmit data is becoming
more important. Given that networks will continue to develop along the
lines suggested, with combinations of mini-processors at various levels
performing both control and applications functions, the role of the
central large-scale computer diminishes towards that of a filing clerk.
This implies that the impressive data communications control packages
developed during the days of idiot networks are obsolescent. Do you
need multithreading on medium-scale systems when the input has been
reduced to a trickle of 'clean' messages few of which require a fast
response? What price QTAM or TCAM now that a front-end performs the
queueing for you? (Perhaps making a 100-terminal network look like a
card reader?) None of these things is likely unless minicomputer software improves radically. However, I believe that these improvements will
occur and many changes in mainframe communications software are in the
offing.

QUESTIONS, DISCUSSION TOPICS AND ASSIGNMENTS

1. What are the main features of minicomputers which cause us to
   classify them separately from small-scale general purpose machines?
   Which of these features are most relevant to data communications
   systems?

2. As mentioned in Chapter 9, the usefulness of minis in data communications is still very much dependant upon the quality of

163

software available. What software features would you look for
when evaluating mini-processors for inclusion in:

(a) An intelligent interactive terminal

(b) A remote store-and-forward concentrator

(c) A front-end processor.

CHAPTER 10

DATA TRANSMISSION FACILITIES IN EUROPE

Our discussion of data communications techniques has, so far, been
of a generalised nature. However, the structure, policy outlook and
technical restrictions of each telecommunications authority varies quite
significantly from country to country in Europe. It is not possible
within the scope of one book, to document all these national differences
in an adequate amount of detail. Furthermore, the European scene is
changing so rapidly that there is no guarantee that any statement made
in this chapter at the time of writing will still be valid when the book
is published. If the reader is likely to be involved in the installation
of data transmission systems in any of the European countries mentioned,
he is strongly advised to check all details with the relevant PTT first -
this section of the book is intended as a guide only. Even in the case
of the U.K. where the Post Office services are described in considerable
detail, it is strongly recommended that all crucial facts be checked with
the Corporation before finalising any teleprocessing plans. The person
to write to in the first instance is the Telephone Manager of your local
area. Specifically, included in this chapter will be information on the
availability of data communications services within each major European
country, the use of international circuits, Post Office Corporation (POC)
facilities in the U.K. and future developments in data transmission.

10.1   THE EUROPEAN SCENE

In order to carry out a meaningful comparison of the services offered
by each national PTT it is necessary to establish what might be considere
as a 'standard' range of facilities that the designer of online systems
might look for. Table 10.1 shows such a possible selection.
The extent to which each country provides such a range is shown in
Table 10.2. Particular attention needs to be paid to the regulations
concerning the use of modems. The following situations exist:

1. The PTT does not supply modems but any used must receive prior approval from the PTT.

2. The PTT requires that its own modems be used on switched networks but any *approved* modem may be used on dedicated circuits (including those which might be supplied by the PTT itself).

3. Either PTT supplied or other approved modems may be used on switched or dedicated lines.

4. Only PTT supplied modems can be used.

In some countries (e.g. Sweden and Switzerland), the use of acoustical couplers is banned.

The extent to which the performance of circuits is guaranteed by the PTT also varies. For example, in the U.K. a speed of 600 bits/sec on switched telephone lines is guaranteed, although speeds of 1200 or even 2400 can be achieved (the latter mainly being dependant upon the modem used and the standard of the relevant local exchange). Other countries provide circuits conditioned to CCITT M111 or M102 specification, leaving the user to obtain the maximum performance required through the judicious use of modems. Denmark, however, will make no guarantees about the performance of its leased lines.

Table 10.1   *Possible 'standard' range of data transmission facilities*

Circuit Type	Switched (bits/sec)	Dedicated (bits/sec)
Telegraph	50 (TELEX)	50,75,100 or 200
Telephone	Up to 300 asynchronous Up to 1200 asynchronous Up to 4800 (HDX) synchronous	Up to 1200 asynchronous Up to 9600 synchronous
Wideband	48k (manually switched)	48k 240k
Digital	Packet Switching or up to 9600 Circuit Switching	Up to 240k

Table 10.2   *Availability of Data Transmission facilities in some European Countries*

		Telex	Leased telegraph lines	Public switched network	Leased telephone lines	Broadband channels	Modems
		bits/sec	bits/sec	bits/sec	bits/sec or standard	kHz	
SWITZER-LAND	normal	50	50,200	600	1200	48	PTT modems mandatory for PSN Acoustic couplers not allowed
	possible			1200 2400	2400 4800 (special lines)		
ITALY	normal	50	50,100,200	1200	CCITT M58 CCITT M102		PTT supplies in some modems (200,600,1200 bits/sec)
	possible future						
BELGIUM	normal	50	50,70,100, 200	1200 (data) (limit)	CCITT M58	48	None from PTT at present but modems will be available in the future (200,600 bits/sec).There is a modem tax when PSN is used
	possible future	200	2				

Table 10.2 continued

Country		50	50,100,200	1200 (600 guaranteed) 2400	CCITT M102		Remarks
NETHER-LANDS	normal	50	50,100,200	1200 (600 guaranteed)	CCITT M102	10	None from PTT but approval of modems is necessary
	possible future			2400		48	
UNITED KINGDOM	normal	50	50,100 (tariffs H/J)	1200	1200 (tariff S3) 2400 (tariff T i.e. CCITT M102)	48	PO modems only for switched networks
	possible			2400	up to 9600	240	Other modems available but approved private modems may be used.(200,600, 1200,2400,48000 bits/sec from PTT)
	future			4800 (by 1975)			Experimental packet-switched services being planned for 1975. Digital Data Services to be installed by early 1980
FRANCE	normal	50	50,200	no restrictions	2400 (CCITT M102)	48	None from PTT but approval of modems is necessary.CADUCEE system installed for data transmission purposes.
	possible future				up to 9600	240	

Table 10.2 continued

Country						Remarks
GERMANY	normal	50 (200 with DATEX)	50,100,200	1200 (DATEL)	CCITT M58 / CCITT	10 / 48 / 240	Modems from PTT
	possible future	EDS		2400	9600		
DENMARK	normal	50	50,100,200	1200	600,1200	48	PTT supplied some modems
	possible				nothing guaranteed	240	
	future	(under consideration)		2400 (possibly in 1974)			
SWEDEN	normal	50	50,100,200	1200	CCITT M102		PTT modems available but private modems may be used. (200,600,1200, 2400 bits/sec from PTT) Acoustic couplers not allowed
	possible				3600		
	future			2400 (under test)	4800 (under test)		

169

10.2 INTERNATIONAL DATA TRANSMISSION

With the growth in international trade in general, and the expansion of the European Economic Community in particular, the transmission of data across national boundaries is becoming increasingly important. More and more companies are operating on an international or even multinational basis and many terminals are now being installed to help allay the geographical difficulties of such operations. A good range of international data communications facilities are available between most European countries as shown in Table 10.3.

Table 10.3 *International Data Transmission Facilities*

Telegraph
50 bits/sec on Telex
 	
Up to 100 bits/sec
on leased circuits
	•International Datel 100 provides
	  50 bits/sec on the Telex network
	
	•Leased lines can provide working
	  at 50, 75 or 100 bits/sec

Telephone
200 (FDX), 600 or 1200
bits/sec (HDX) on
switched lines.
Up to 9600 bits/sec
(FDX) on leased
lines.
	•International Datel 200 provides
	  FDX 200 bits/sec rates on the
	  switched public telephone network
	  (dialled on ISD or operator
	  connected).
	•International Datel 600 provides
	  HDX 1200 bits/sec or 600 bits/sec
	  on switched public telephone
	  network (dialled on ISD or operator
	  connected).
	•Leased speech circuits are also
	  available in either standard or
	  conditioned quality giving trans-
	  mission at rates of up to 9600
	  bits/sec depending on the modems
	  used.

Wideband
40k bits/sec
	•48 kHz wideband circuits can be
	  provided between some countries
	  but usually at long notice.
	•40k bits/sec is normally the
	  maximum speed attainable

Because most countries require the use of PTT-supplied modems on the public switched networks, international data communications which make use of dialled or operator connected lines are provided under the name of 'International Datel Services'. These services include the provision

of modems and exchange lines or, in the case of telegraph transmission,
the terminal equipment.

International Datel 100 involves the use of standard teleprinter
equipment (commonly with paper tape facilities) on the Telex network
at a speed of 50 bits (6·67 characters) per second.
International Datel 200 calls are made on the telephone network
using International Subscriber Dialling (ISD) or operator connected lines.
Transmission normally takes place at 200 bits/sec (but 300 bits/sec may
sometimes be possible), in a full duplex mode.

International Datel 600 is a similar service, but the modems provided
allow for transmission to take place at 600 bits/sec or, if the quality
of the line permits, at a maximum of 1200 bits/sec (half-duplex only).

Table 10.4   *Charges for speech calls (selection of countries only)*

COUNTRY	DIALLED DIRECT		OPERATOR CONNECT	
	Seconds per 1p	Cost per minute	Seconds per 1p	Cost per minute
Belgium	5.14	11.67p	4	15p
France	5.14	11.67p	4	15p
Luxembourg	5.14	11.67p	4	15p
The Netherlands	5.14	11.67p	4	15p
Monaco	5.14	11.67p	4	15p
Germany	4.00	15.00p	3.3	18p
Switzerland	4.00	15.00p	3.3	18p
Italy	3.6	16.67p	3.0	20p
Norway	3.00	20.00p	2.6	23p
U.S.A (Lond-NY)	1.20	50.00p	0.8	75p
Austria	-	-	3	20p
Denmark	-	-	3.3	18p
Finland	-	-	1.7	35p
Greece	-	-	1.5	40p
Malta	-	-	1.6	37p
Spain/Portugal	-	-	2.1	28p
Sweden	-	-	2.6	23p
Japan	-	-	0.7	83p
Hong Kong	-	-	0.48	125p
Australia	—	-	0.6	100p

The 200 and 600 services make use of Post Office Modems No. 2 and 1
respectively at a rental of £100 p.a. in each case. Both these devices
are described in more detail later in this chapter. The charges for the
circuits are the same as those for a speech call to Continental countries

171

(a higher charge is applied to Intercontinental calls) and a selection
of the normal telephone rates is shown in Table 10.4. Rates for countries
not shown here may be obtained from Post Office Booklet PG 272 which can
be obtained from the Sales Office of your local Telephone Manager. Although
the rates do not change too frequently, the countries which can be dialled
directly on ISD are always increasing and the rate for such calls is lower
than for operator connected circuits.

It may be apparent that the modems used for International Datel links
could present problems. Although British Post Office modems are constructed
to international standards, there is no guarantee that those available in
the country being called will be 100% compatible. Similarly, technical
problems may occur with the matching of suitable telegraph equipment. For
these reasons (and others of a political and administrative nature) the
three services are not universally available to all countries. Table 10.5
indicates the position as it was in mid-1973, but it is of course, advisable
for you to check the current position with the Post Office.

Two types of international leased lines are available.The first is a
standard speech circuit which confirms to CCITT M111. The performance
obtainable from an M111 line depends very much on the modems used (and how
much you want to pay for them). A speed of 1200 bits/sec should be easily
attainable, but some companies supply modems specifically designed to
achieve rates of 2400 or even 4800 from these circuits. In addition,
'special quality' lines conditioned to meet CCITT M102, can be obtained
and these will handle speeds of up to 9600 bits/sec with little difficulty.
It is generally necessary to acquire modems from non-PTT sources for international leased telephone lines although any such modems used will, of
course, need to be approved by the national telecommunications authorities
concerned. Most international networks are point-to-point only. Lines
can be interconnected to provide some form of multidropping, but the
relevant PTTs may then no longer guarantee the qualities of the circuits
used. In addition, leased telegraph circuits can be installed for use
with the customer's own terminal equipment. Lines capable of handling
rates of 200 bits/sec can be provided but in most countries telegraph
equipment typically works at speeds of 50, 75 or 110 bits/sec. The
method of charging for international leased circuits conforms to a
somewhat complex set of rules agreed by the Conference of European
Postal and Telecommunications Administrations (CEPT), and the CCITT.
For intra-European circuits 'standard rental charge' is calculated on
the basis of 9,000 minutes per month of the total through accounting
rate for a telephone call (ISD) between the two countries involved.

Table 10.5 *Availability of International Datel Services*

Country	Datel Service		
	100	200	600
Algeria	×		
Australia			×
Austria			×
Bahrain		×	×
Balearic Islands		×	
Belgium	×	×	×
Canada			×
Denmark	×		×
Dubai		×	×
Finland	×	×	×
France	×	×	×
Germany	×	×	×
Greece	×		
Hong Kong			×
Hungary	×		
Italy	×		
Luxembourg	×		
Netherlands	×	×	×
Norway	×	×	×
Poland	×		
Portugal	×		
Spain (Madrid)		×	×
Sweden	×		×
Switzerland	×	×	×
U.S.A. via ITT		×	×
via RCA		×	×
via WUI		×	×
Yugoslavia	×		

This standard charge is then adjusted by various 'multiplication co-efficients', surcharges and discounts, according to the exact type of circuit needed and the way in which it will be used (see Figure 10.1). As the rentals charged can be paid at either end in most cases, these need to be converted into the appropriate local currency. This is done through a 'notional' currency known as 'gold francs' which is updated every week to allow for the frequent fluctuations in currency exchange rates. It is impossible, therefore, to provide any kind of accurate quotation of the prevailing costs of such leased lines. To make matters even more complicated for the systems analyst designing a European Network, national PTTs tend to know very little about the availability of circuits which do not involve their own countries.

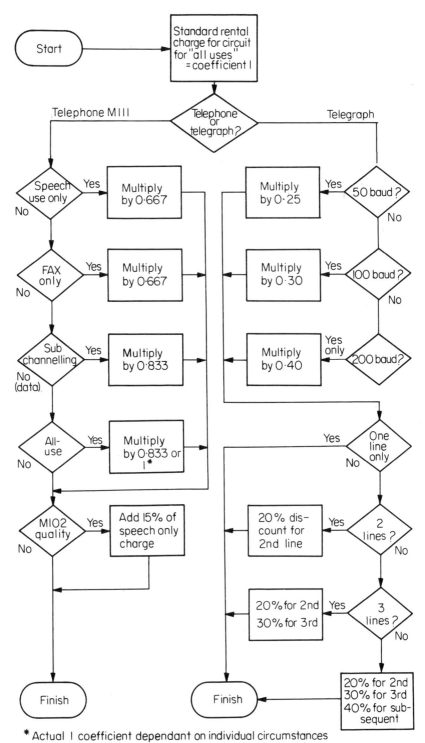

* Actual I coefficient dependant on individual circumstances

Figure 10.1. Method of charging for international leased circuits

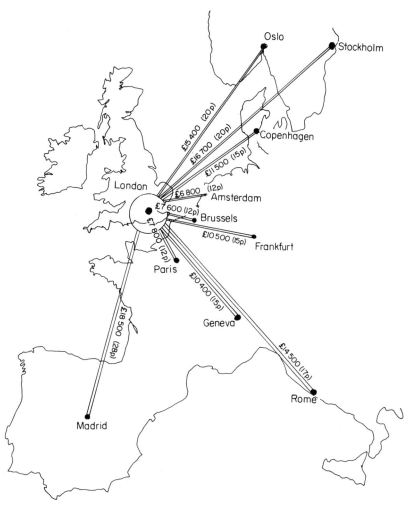

Figure 10.2. Approximate annual rental charges for a selection of
international leased speech-only circuits (Mlll) from
the U.K. to other European countries (Courtesy:
International Communications Systems Consultants Ltd.)

Notes

1. Overall sterling rental charges shown are those
    applying as at 1 September 1972. (Since that date
    a percentage increase would apply - revised quarterly -
    in respect of foreign shares collected in the U.K.
    while the pound remains 'floating')

2. Rental charges have been rounded up to the nearest
    £100

3. Figures shown in brackets are per minute. Charges
    for ISD telephone calls from the U.K. rounded to
    the nearest whole penny. (Spain is operator connected)

Table 10.6   European approximate annual rental charges for a typical selection of leased speech-only circuits (M111) indicated by Pounds Sterling, rounded up to the nearest £100

(By courtesy of International Communications Systems Limited)

APPROXIMATE OVERALL RENTAL £ p.a.	Amsterdam	Brussels	Copen-hagen	Frankfurt	Geneva	London	Madrid	Oslo	Paris	Rome	Stockholm
Amsterdam	5,300										
Copenhagen	6,800	8,500									
Frankfurt	9,200	8,000	9,100								
Geneva	8,700	9,300	10,600	10,000							
* London	6,800	7,600	11,500	12,500	10,400						
Madrid	17,600	16,500		21,300	17,000	18,500					
Oslo	9,800	9,900	3,400	12,600	13,190	15,400					
Paris	7,400	7,200	10,200	11,000	8,500	7,800	14,400	12,300			
Rome	9,900	13,000	13,700	14,600	10,900	14,500	21,100	16,800	13,200		
Stockholm	9,900	12,200	4,500	12,500	14,000	16,700	23,600	3,300	13,400	17,700	

* Overall sterling rental charges shown above are those applying as at 1 September 1972 (since that date a percentage increase would apply (revised quarterly) in respect of foreign shares collected in the U.K. while the Pound remains 'floating'.)

A London based company, International Communications Systems Consultants
Limited (I.C.S.C.), have an online database of tariff information which
is updated frequently with variables such as the current Gold Franc
rate and regulatory charges. Simply by entering on a terminal the
type of circuit required and the countries to be connected, an accurate
indication of the charges can be produced with conversions into local
currencies and into sterling for project costing purposes. Both Figure
10.2 and Table 10.6 were prepared by I.C.S.C.

In order to give an indication of the charges made for leased circuits
from the U.K. to a number of other European countries, some approximate
annual rentals for M111 (normal quality) speech only circuits are shown
in Figure 10.2. The figures shown in brackets are the charges per minute
for dialled (ISD) telephone calls from the U.K. to the countries indicated.
(These are also the charges for International Datel 200 and 600 calls from
the U.K.). Table 10.6 goes further to show, on a matrix basis, the cost
of M111 speech only circuits between eleven European countries.

The reader is urged to obtain a copy of CEPT Draft Recommendation
T/PGT10 to become acquainted with the varied and complex rules of international data communications, if he is going to get involved in that area.

10.3   DATA TRANSMISSION IN THE U.K.

In Great Britain the Post Office Corporation is the monopoly supplier
of telecommunications facilities. Although it is possible to lease
circuits for use with any type of equipment permitted for connection by
the Post Office, the Corporation 'packages' certain of its data transmission facilities under the term 'Datel Services'. 'Datel' is a
contraction of *DA*ta *TEL*ecommunications. Those services include the
provision of a circuit and, where appropriate, suitable modems. The
current range of Datel Services are :

Datel 100

Datel 200

Datel 400

Datel 600

Datel 2400

Datel 2400 dial-up

Datel 48k

Other services and facilities available in the U.K. which will be described
in this chapter are:

Table 10.7   *Summary of Post Office Datel Services*

Service	Modem	SPTN		Leased		
		Mode	Speed (bits/sec)	Mode	Speed (bits/sec)	Tariff
Datel 100	None (Telegraph)		50 (Telex)		50 110	H J
Datel 200	No. 2 (asynch)	FDX	Up to 300 (200 assured)	FDX	Up to 300 (200 assured)	Sl
Datel 400	No.10 (asynch)		Data Acquisition Service			
Datel 600	No. 1 (asynch)	HDX	600 (as main circuit or as backup to leased line) + 75 supervisory channels	HDX FDX	600 (2-wire circuits) 600 or 1200 4-wire circuits + 75 supervisory channels	Sl S3
Datel 2400	No.7B	HDX	600 or 1200	FDX	2400 plus 72 supervisory channels	T
Datel 2400 Dial-up	No.7C	HDX	2400 1200 600		PSTN Rates	
Datel 48k	No. 8		Withdrawn	FDX	40,800 48,000 50,000	Rates by special quotation

178

Data control equipments

Midnight line service

Dataplex services.

The main features of the Datel Services are listed in Table 10.7. Notice that it is not possible to *buy* Post Office equipment of any kind. The POC claim that by retaining ownership of all units they can ensure that maintenance is at the highest level and that upgrades may be effected when necessary. Maintenance charges are included in the rental.

10.3.1 Datel 100

This service started in 1964 and in 1973 had nearly 3,000 users. Telegraph communication facilities are used and speeds available are 50 bits/sec on the Telex Switched network and up to 110 bits/sec on leased lines. Post Office supplied teleprinters (which can incorporate paper-tape facilities) can be used at speeds up to 75 bits/sec (50 bits/sec on Telex) based upon International Alphabet No. 2. Privately supplied equipment may be used if higher speeds or alternative codes (e.g. IA5) are needed. The service is particularly useful for systems involving keyboard input and low volume printed output. Table 10.8 lists the Post Office charges for the various items of telegraph equipment which it offers.

Table 10.8 *Charges for Post Office supplied telegraph equipment (as at September 1973)*

DATEL 100	Annual Rental	Connection Charge
Telex: Teleprinter (with pt facilities)	£360	£23
Teleprinter No. 15 with pt facilities	£370	£15
Private Circuits: Teleprinter No.15	£220	£10
Autotape transmitter	£70	£10
Teleprinter No.15 - with pt read/punch 50/bits/sec	£280	£10
with pt read/punch 75 bits/sec	£350	£10
Teleprinter: 'All 5 unit Codes' Modification	£9	–
Error detection unit	£120	£10
UTX 7	£20	–
Character recognition unit	£125	£10
Circuits: 50 bits/sec	see Tariff H	
Up to 110 bits/sec	see Tariff J (Bulk Tariffs also available)	

Table 10.9 *Datel 100 Tariffs H and J* (as at September 1973)

Chargeable length or circuit	Tariff H (50 bits/sec)	Tariff J (Up to 110 bits/sec)	Connection charge
	£.p.a.	£.p.a.	£
0-1	7	7	
Over 1 up to 2 Furlongs	13	13	8
" 2-3 longs	19	19	
" 3-4	22	22	
" 4-6	28	28	
" 6-8	34	34	
" 1-$1\frac{1}{4}$ miles	37	37	
" $1\frac{1}{4}$-$1\frac{1}{2}$ "	41	41	
" $1\frac{1}{2}$-$1\frac{3}{4}$ "	46	46	
" $1\frac{3}{4}$-2 "	50	50	
" 2-$2\frac{1}{2}$ "	56	56	
" $2\frac{1}{2}$-3 "	64	64	
" 3-4 "	76	76	15
" 4-5 "	92	92	
" 5-6 "	108	108	
" 6-8 "	132	132	
" 8-10 "	165	165	
" 10-12 "	265	265	
" 12-14 "	265	265	
" 14-16 "	265	265	
" 16-18 "	265	265	
" 18-20 "	265	265	
" 20-22 "	375	415	20
" 22-24 "	375	415	
" 24-26 "	375	415	
" 26-28 "	375	415	
" 28-30 "	375	415	
" 30-35 "	385	485	
" 35-40 "	385	485	
" 40-45 "	395	525	25
" 45-50 "	395	525	
" 50-60 "	405	545	
" 60-70 "	415	555	
" 70-80 "	420	565	30
" 80-90 "	425	575	
" 90-100 "	435	585	
" 100-150 "	450	645	
" 150-180	475	685	
" 180-200 "	475	685	
" 200-250 "	495	705	35
" 250-300 "	515	735	
" 300 "	535	755	

Table 10.10   *DATEL 100 Bulk Tariffs H and J* (as at September 1973)

Chargeable length of circuit	Bulk tariff H 6	12	18	24	Bulk tariff J 6 circuits	12 circuits
	£	£	£	£	£	£
Up to 22 miles	825	1,075	1,375	1,850	880	1,300
Over 22 miles up to 24 miles	855	1,105	1,405	1,890	920	1,340
" 24 " " " 26 "	885	1,135	1,435	1,930	960	1,380
" 26 " " " 28 "	915	1,165	1,465	1,970	1,000	1,420
" 28 " " " 30 "	945	1,195	1,495	2,010	1,040	1,460
" 30 " " " 35 "	1,015	1,265	1,565	2,090	1,120	1,560
" 35 " " " 40 "	1,070	1,320	1,620	2,190	1,180	1,640
" 40 " " " 45 "	1,125	1,375	1,675	2,270	1,240	1,720
" 45 " " " 50 "	1,180	1,430	1,730	2,350	1,300	1,800
" 50 " " " 60 "	1,290	1,540	1,840	2,480	1,410	1,930
" 60 " " " 70 "	1,400	1,650	1,950	2,610	1,520	2,060
" 70 " " " 80 "	1,510	1,760	2,060	2,740	1,630	2,190
" 80 " " " 90 "	1,620	1,870	2,170	2,870	1,740	2,320
" 90 " " " 100 "	1,730	1,980	2,80	3,000	1,850	2,450
" 100 " " " 120 "	1,840	2,090	2,390	3,110	1,960	2,560
" 120 " " " 140 "	1,990	2,240	2,540	3,260	2,110	2,710
" 140 " " " 160 "	2,140	2,390	2,690	3,410	2,260	2,860
" 160 " " " 180 "	2,290	2,540	2,840	3,560	2,410	3,010
" 180 " " " 200 "	2,440	2,690	2,990	3,710	2,560	3,160
" 200 " " " 250 "	2,640	2,660	3,260	3,980	2,820	3,420
" 250 " " " 300 "	2,840	3,290	3,590	4,310	3,160	3,760
" 300 miles	3,000	3,590	3,890	4,610	3,460	4,060

CONNECTION CHARGES

On both bulk tariffs, irrespective of chargeable length of circuits, the connection charges will be as follows:

1. Initial installations

   (a) 6 or 12 circuit groups - £250

   (b) 18 or 24 circuit groups - £400

2. Additions of extra groups of circuits subsequent to the initial installation will have a connection charge as follows:

   | Extension of 6 circuit group to 12 circuit group £ 50 |
   | "   "   6   "   "   " 18   "   " £150 |
   | "   "   6   "   "   " 24   "   " £150 |
   | "   "   12   "   "   " 18   "   " £150 |
   | "   "   12   "   "   " 24   "   " £150 |
   | "   "   18   "   "   " 24   "   " £ 50 |

There will be no charge when an additional circuit within a group of 6 is taken into use (eg 10 circuits to 11 circuits).

Where the public network is being used, normal Telex charges apply according to distance as follows:

Up to 35 miles	60 sec for 1p
Between 35 and 75 miles	30 sec for 1p
Over 75 miles	15 sec for 1p

If the line being used is leased from the Post Office, the annual charge will depend upon the length of the line and speed for which it is suitable. For 50 bits/sec working Tariff H is applicable. Tariff J is used for speeds of up to 110 bits /sec. Both the tariffs are shown in full in Table 10.9. Note that a connection charge is applicable. Should the customer wish to connect a number of devices all in one location to a central point, a significant discount is available in the form of Bulk Tariffs. Table 10.10 illustrates the rates applicable when groups of 6, 12 (H and J), 18 and 24 (H only) circuits are used.

10.3.2 Datel 200

This service started in 1967 and in 1973 had about 10,000 users.

Table 10.11   *DATEL 200 Alternative Line Arrangements*

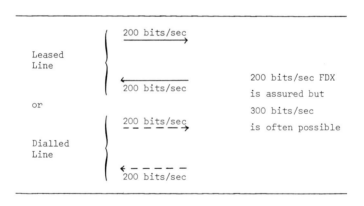

The telephone network is used and lines may be leased or dialled (Table 10.11). The Post Office supplies Modem No. 2 as part of this service. The speed is assured up to 200 bits/sec, but it has been found that in most cases it is possible to operate at 300 bits/sec. Most acoustical couplers are designed to be compatible with Modem No. 2 in such a way that the couplers at remote locations can dial up the centrally situated modems. Datel 200 is the service normally used to connect interactive terminals to time-sharing services on the switched public telephone net-

work. Full duplex working is available but, because two-wire circuits
are used, it is not normally possible to multidrop terminals on single
dedicated lines. If required, the modem can be arranged to answer calls
automatically in conjunction with suitable terminal equipment. Dialled
calls are charged at normal STD or operator connected rates. Leased
lines are charged according to the radial distance between the end of
the circuit on Tariff S1 which is shown in Table 10.12. Modem No. 2 rents
for £100 p.a.

10.3.3 Datel 400

This service is designed for telemetry systems and other data
acquisition applications. It is assumed that such applications are
outside the reader's immediate area of interest and are not, therefore
included here. However, your local Post Office General Manager's Sales
Office will be able to provide further details and assistance.

10.3.4 Datel 600

This service started in 1966 and some 12,000 terminals were installed
by the end of 1973 (mostly with the clearing banks). A start-stop modem
(No. 1) is used and transmission on leased lines is assured up to 1200
bits/sec and on the SPN up to 600 bits/sec (Table 10.13). On some dialled
circuits it is possible to achieve speeds of 1200 bits/sec, but this will
vary from exchange to exchange. Line arrangements incorporating 75 bits/sec
supervisory channels are possible. SPN Calls are, of course, chargeable at
normal speech rates. Line arrangements 1, 2 and 3 in Table 10.13 may be
implemented using Tariff S1 quality lines, if a speed of 600 bits/sec only
is required. In all other cases, i.e. where assured 1200 bits/sec operation
and/or full duplex working is needed, 4-wire S3 circuits must be used
(Table 10.12).

Where S3 lines are to be used these can be installed in multipoint
configurations if required. A maximum of 3 links in tandem and 12
outstations is permissible (Figure 10.3).

The method of costing Datel 600 multipoint circuits is as follows:

1. Measure the radial distance between the computer centre and
    the first branching point.
2. Measure the radial distance between the first branching
    point and the second branching point (if any).
3. Measure the radial length of each spur.
4. Use Tariff S3 to obtain the annual rental for each of the
    sections measured in 1., 2. and 3. and sum.

183

Table 10.12 *Post Office Speech Tariffs S1, S2, S3 and T*
(as at September, 1973)
(see P.O. Document X1997 for further details)

Chargeable length of circuit		S1 £.p.a.		S2 £.p.a.		S3 £.p.a.		T £.p.a.		Connection charge
		£ (a)	(b)	£ (a)	(b)	£ (a)	(b)	£ (a)	(b)	£
0-1		7	10	7	10	14	17	16	19	
Over 1 up to 2		13	16	13	16	26	29	31	34	
" 2-3		19	22	19	22	38	41	45	48	8
" 3 4	furlongs	22	25	22	25	44	41	53	56	
" 4-6			30		30		56		67	
" 6-8			34		34		68		79	
" 1-1¼ miles			37		37		74		87	
" 1¼-1½ "			41		41		82		97	
" 1½-1¾ "			46		47		92		109	
" 1¾-2 "			50		52		100		119	
" 2-2½ "			56		60		112		134	
" 2½-3 "			64		72		128		152	15
" 3-4 "			76		90		152		179	
" 4-5 "			92		114		184		214	
" 5-6 "			108		140		210		242	
" 6-8 "			132		170		240		274	
" 8-10 "			165		211		282		313	
" 10-12 "			265		335		410		420	
" 12-14 "			265		335		410		420	
" 14-16 "			265		335		410		420	
" 16-18 "			265		335		410		420	
" 18-20 "			265		335		410		420	
" 20-22 "			415		515		610		620	20
" 22-24 "			415		515		610		620	
" 24-26 "			415		515		610		620	
" 26-28 "			415		515		610		620	
" 28-30 "			415		515		610		620	
" 30-35 "			525		655		730		750	
" 35-40 "			525		655		730		750	30
" 40-45 "			625		785		840		910	
" 45-50 "			625		785		840		910	
" 50-60 "			745		845		900		1010	
" 60-70 "			845		945		1000		1120	
" 70-80 "			935		1035		1090		1250	40
" 80-90 "			985		1145		1200		1360	
" 90-100 "			1065		1235		1290		1460	
" 100-150 "			1300		1535		1570		1710	50
" 150-160 "			1595		1795		1850		2010	
" 160-180 "			1595		1795		1850		2010	
" 180-200 "			1595		1795		1850		2010	
" 200-250 "			1810		1995		2040		2200	
" 250-300 "			2065		2195		2310		2500	
" 300 "			2355		2495		2560		2780	

N.B: This approach gives an approximation of costs only; the Post Office reserve the right to site branching points at locations most favourable from the viewpoint of service arrangements and their own plant availability. Also, additional annual charges are imposed for reconditioning lines etc. Connection charges are based upon the total network rental thus:

5% if less than £100,000
3% if greater than £100,000

Modem No.1 rents for £100 p.a. Modems attached to private circuits will be equipped with a telephone handset and an exchange line to facilitate remote testing of the modem. The facility will also enable the public network to be used (perhaps at a lower speed) as backup in case of failure of the main circuit. Automatic answering facilities can be provided.

Table 10.13   *DATEL 600 alternative line arrangements*

	Leased Circuit bits/sec	Switched Network bits/sec
1. Simplex with supervisory	600/1200 ⟶ 75 ⟵	600/1200 ⟶ 75 ⟵
2. Half-Duplex	600/1200 ⟷	600/1200 ⟷
3. Half-Duplex with HDX supervisory channel	600/1200 ⟷ 75 ⟷	600/1200 ⟷ 75 ⟷
4. Full-Duplex	600/1200 ⟶ 600/1200 ⟵	N/A
5. Full-Duplex with supervisory channels	75 ⟵ 600/1200 ⟶ 600/1200 ⟵ 75 ⟶	N/A

185

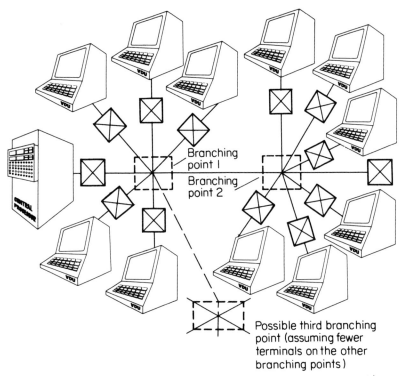

Branching point 1
Branching point 2

Possible third branching point (assuming fewer terminals on the other branching points)

Figure 10.3. Multipoint configuration possible with Tariff S3 quality circuits.

1. Usually one, two or three branching points but no more than two in tandem.

2. Up to twelve spurs but no other restrictions on the numbers attached to each point

Note: Modems are not required at branching points

10.3.5   Datel 2400

Datel 2400 which was announced in 1968 had some 2,400 users by the end of 1973. Transmission can take place in a variety of circuit arrangements (Table 10.14) at speeds of up to 2400 bits/sec. 75 bits/sec supervisory channels can be incorporated and the switched telephone network is available at speeds of 600 or, if possible, 1200 bits/sec for backup purposes. Modem No. 7 is used and transmission takes place in a synchronous fashion on both private lines and the SPN. The 4-wire leased lines must be conditioned to Tariff T which is similar to CCITT M102 Standard (Table 10.12). Such circuits may be point-to-point or multipoint and in the latter case the rules are the same as for Tariff S3 (Figure 10.3), but only *one* branching point is allowed i.e. no more than two links in tandem (Figure 10.4). The same costing guidelines also apply but Modem No. 7 rents for £200 p.a.

Table 10.14   *Datel 2400 alternative line arrangements*

	Leased Line bits/sec	Switched Network (backup only) bits/sec
FDX (no SPN backup)	2400 → ← 2400	N/A
FDX with HDX SPN backup	2400 → ← 2400	← ----- → 600/1200
*FDX with supervisory channels	← 75 2400 → ← 2400 75 →	
*FDX with supervisory channels and FDX SPN working with supervisory channels	← 75 2400 → ← 2400 75 →	(Uses two exchange lines) ← --- 75 ------- → 600/1200 ← ------ 600/1200 --- → 75
Simplex with supervisory (no SPN backup)	2400 → ← 75	N/A
Simplex with supervisory and simplex SPN backup with supervisory	2400 → ← 75	---- → 600/1200 ← ------ 75

*These arrangements will require the use of two modems at each end of the circuit.

187

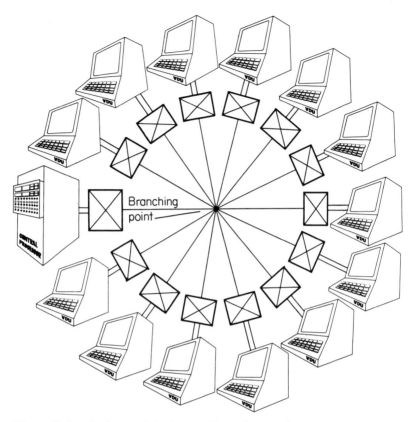

Figure 10.4. Maximum multipoint configuration possible with Tariff T circuits.

1. One branching point
2. No more than two links in tandem
3. Up to twelve outstations

10.3.6 Datel 2400 Dial-up

During the second half of 1972 the Post Office announced the availability of a new version of the synchronous Modem No. 7, (designated 7c), which would enable 2400 bits/sec working on the public telephone network in half-duplex mode. By the end of 1973 there were 40 users and the service looks like being very successful, especially for the temporary connection of remote batch terminals which can benefit from a higher

188

line speed than has been available in the past. However, it should be noted that the Post Office will not guarantee that service will be usable from all locations and offer a one month's trial during which the service can be cancelled without waiting for the end of the normal minimum term of one year. The new modem rents at £280 p.a. plus a £50 connection charge and calls are charged at normal rates.

10.3.7   Datel 48k

This is a wideband service offering speeds of 48,000, 40,800 and 50,000 bits/sec. The 'lines' used are equivalent to 12 speech circuits. Leased connections are available between most major towns. The Post Office admits that Datel 48k has not been particularly successful to date owing, possibly, to the high cost involved and the development of suitable applications. A tariff is not available and the Post Office quotes separately for each circuit. However, a 25 mile one way link could cost in the region of £3,000 p.a. and a 250 mile two way line over £20,000 p.a. Much of the cost is in the provision of 'local ends' between the exchanges and the customer's premises. In some areas the Post Office is able to provide circuits which will operate at speeds up to 240,000 bits sec.

10.4   DATA CONTROL EQUIPMENTS

The Post Office supplies three types of 'Data Control Equipments'; DCE1, DCE2 and DCE3. The Corporation's predeliction for putting 'data' in front of everything not concerned with speech communications can be confusing. The DCEs are concerned with the control of circuits not data!

10.4.1   Automatic calling (telephone network):   DCE1

DCE1 is used for the automatic origination of calls on the switched public telephone network in conjunction with PO Modems No. 1, 2 or 7. The terminal being called can be manually connected or, alternatively, use can be made of the automatic answering facilities incorporated in the modem. The calling unit, whether a computer or a terminal, needs to incorporate an additional interface to control the DCE. The data interface is the standard CCITT V.24 25-pin cable (*see* Chapter 4 and Appendix 1). Once the connection is made, this is used in exactly the same way as any other modem interface; the DCE1 is transparent. The additional 25-pin interface cable has been added to enable the computer (or terminal) to pass the digits of the number being called to the DCE. This is done in binary fashion on four of the circuits. The circuits are allocated according to the '200' series of V.24 specification.

189

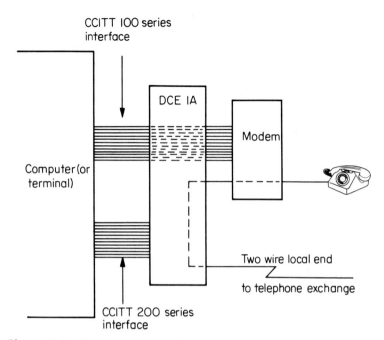

Figure 10.5. Data control equipment No. 1A (DCE1A)

Figure 10.5 shows the arrangement of the various components. Table 10.15 indicates the assignment of circuits to the interface pins. The sequence of operation is as follows:

1. If the computer wishes to make a call it checks that the DCE1 power is on (213) and that the line is not busy (203).
2. If OK, then the computer indicates that it wishes to place a call (202).
3. The DCE will then request the first digit of the number (210).
4. The computer puts the binary value of the first digit of the number on the signal circuits (206 to 209) and tells the DCE that it is there (211).
5. The DCE interprets the number and concerts it to conventional dial pulses. In addition to the digits 0-9 two other codes can be passed: SEP, Separation and EON, End of number. The first is used where a time delay might be required. For example, if the DCE is connected to a PABX it might be necessary to dial '9' in order to obtain an exchange line and the dial tone will not occur immediately thus requiring the insertion of at least

190

one SEP.

After the pulses have been sent, the DCE requests the next digit (210).

Table 10.15 *DCE1A Calling Interface*

CCITT Circuit number	Circuit	Pin number
201	Signal Ground	7
202	Call Request	4
203	Data Line Occupied	22
204	Distant Station Connected	13
205	Abandon Call	3
206	Data Signal Circuit (2^0)	14
207	Data Signal Circuit (2^1)	15
208	Data Signal Circuit (2^2)	16
209	Data Signal Circuit (2^3)	17
210	Present Next Digit	5
211	Digit Present	2
213	Power Indication	6

6. The computer continues to present digits as per 3 to 5 and finishes with EON.

7. If the DCE successfully establishes the connection it tells the computer (204) and connects the modem to the line. If the call fails i.e. if the distant modem carrier is not received within a period of up to 40 sec, then the DCE indicates 'Abandon Call' (205).

The timing of this operation is quite critical and reference should be made to the relevant PO document; Technical Guide No. 8.

10.4.2 Automatic answering (telephone network): DCE2

DCE2A is designed according to the CCITT Recommendation V.25 to work in conjunction with Modems Nos. 1, 2 or 7 to automatically answer calls received from the switched public telephone network (especially international calls). The call may be originated automatically (via DCE1A or foreign equivalent) or manually. The DCE2 is equipped to disable

191

echo suppressors by placing a 2100 Hz signal on the line for 3-5 sec.
A telephone set is supplied with the unit and this can be used to answer
calls manually (a DATA button connects the modem to the line). Otherwise an AUTO ANS button on the top can be depressed causing the DCE2 to
handle calls.

Unlike DCE1, the automatic answering equipment only required one
interface cable. This is because the CCITT interface V.24 includes
the circuits needed for auto-answering (*see* Appendix 1). Figure 10.6
shows the arrangement of the components.

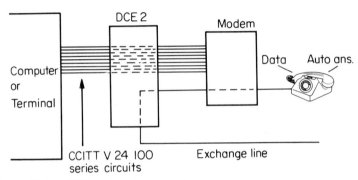

Figure 10.6. DCE2A automatic answering

10.4.3   Automatic calling and answering (Telex network):   DCE3

DCE3 is provided for the automatic reception of calls on the Telex
network. It can be supplied with a Dial Unit No. 901A for the automatic
origination of calls. As with DCE1 and DCE2 the interface is implemented
using the relevant V.24 100-series and 200-series circuits and the functions performed are essentially the same. P.O. Technical Guide No. 10
provides full details of the service.

10.5   MIDNIGHT LINE FACILITY

The Midnight Line Facility is a well conceived but much under used
service with considerable potential in certain application areas. For
a fixed annual rate of £200 the Post Office will provide one exchange
line on which an unlimited number of dialled calls to any U.K. number
can be made between mignight and 6.00 a.m. When used in conjunction
with DCE1 for automatic calling from a computer centre and automatic
answering facilities at the remote locations it can be a very cheap
and efficient method of data collection. The limitation to data has

been on the supply of suitable terminals but more of these are now
coming onto the market. Data is often collected during the day by
recording it on, for example, a magnetic tape cassette. The cassette
is then loaded into a terminal when staff leave the remote location
at the end of their working day. Sometime after midnight the SPN link
will be established automatically and the data transmitted to the central
site. This technique is being used by some stores and shops for stock-
control purposes. The service can, of course, be used for manual call
set-up and more than one 'midnight line' installed should volumes require
it.

10.6 DATAPLEX SERVICES

Chapter 7 described the use of multiplexors and the types which are
generally available. The Post Office now supplies two types of multiplexor under the names DATAPLEX 1 and 2. In 1973 a new regulation was
introduced under which the use of Post Office supplied multiplexors is
obligatory, if connection to the units is to be made over the public
switched network. This rule will only be waived if the user can convince
the Post Office that the multiplexors he wishes to use do essential things
that the DATAPLEX service cannot. If leased lines are used through the
network then privately supplied multiplexors may be acquired. Table 10.16
summarises the capabilities of each DATAPLEX service. Rental charges
are not published but are provided on a 'quotation' basis. Where necessary, modems are included. The remote units may be installed on PO premises
or customer premises, but the central unit must be in the computer centre.

Table 10.16   *Summary of Dataplex Services*

Service	Speeds	Speed Mix	Capacity
	bits/sec		
DATAPLEX 1 (FDM)	110	110 only	12 channels at 110 bits/sec
DATAPLEX 2 (TDM)	50 75 110 134·5 150 200 300 600 1200	Any 7	Maximum 51 channels at 110 bits/sec (or fewer channels at higher speeds)

10.7   THE FUTURE

During the late 1960s and early 1970s the Post Office commissioned a
number of studies into the feasibility of developing a range of services
which would use digital communications techniques and would provide
customers with a purpose built system for the transmission of data.
Since the CCITT have produced a number of draft recommendations for such
digital data services including:

X2   Suggests a range of User Classes which the Post Office
     are likely to implement as follows:

     Class 1a   100 bits/sec Asynchronous
           1b   200 bits/sec   "
           1c   300 bits/sec   "
     Class 3   600 bits/sec Synchronous
     Class 4   2400 bits/sec   "
     Class 5   9600 bits/sec   "
     Class 6   48k bits/sec   "

X20 Is the recommendation for an asynchronous interface⎞(*see*
X21 Is the recommendation for a synchronous interface ⎠Appendix 2)
     It is currently proposed that the U.K. Digital Data Services
     (DDS) will cover three types of network

     1. Digital Private Circuits (From 1977)
     2. Circuit Switched Network ⎞ (From the
     3. Packet Switched Network   ⎠ early 1980s)

As there is no practical experience in the U.K. of packet switching, the
Post Office have established an Experimental Packet Switched Service
(EPSS) which will commence operations in 1975 with three switching nodes
in London, Manchester and Glasgow.   It is hoped that the EPSS will provide
the Post Office, manufacturers and users with enough working experience
of packet operations to help ensure the success of the Packet Switched DDS.
The facilities and features of the three services are likely to be extensive.   But as CCITT Recommendations are not yet finalised and much technical
development has yet to be undertaken, it is not possible to indicate here
the likely nature of these facilities in any detail.   However, the
reader is recommended to look out for Post Office announcements and
publications about DDS over the next few years.

The IBM 3705 Programmable Communications Controller. *Courtesy IBM United Kingdom Ltd.*

The DEC PDP-11/40 minicomputer. *Courtesy of Digital Equipment*

Cased PO Modems No. 1 mounted in racks (left) with various control and test facilities (right). *Courtesy Post Office Corporation.*

PO Modems without cases rack-mounted at a much higher density than has previously been possible. *Courtesy Post Office Corporation.*

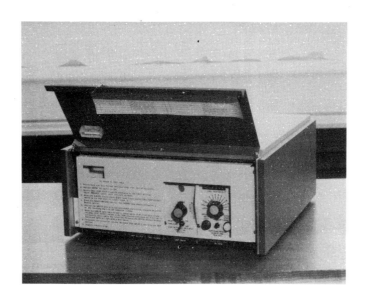

PO DCE 1 Autocalling Unit. *Courtesy Post Office Corporation.*

APPENDIX 1

CCITT Draft Recommendation V.24

I. SCOPE

I.1   This recommendation applies to the interconnecting circuits
being called interchange circuits, at the interface between data terminal
equipment and data communication equipment for the transfer of binary
data, control and timing signals and analogue signals as appropriate.
This recommendation also applies to both sides of separate intermediate
equipment, which may be inserted between these two classes of equipment.

Electrical characteristics for interchange circuits are detailed in
the appropriate Recommendations for Electrical Characteristics, or in
certain special cases, in Recommendations for Data Communication Equipment.

In any type of practical equipment a selection will be made from the
range of interchange circuits defined in this recommendation, as appropriate. When by mutual arrangement other circuits are to be used, these
additional circuits should conform to the electrical characteristics
specified in the appropriate Recommendation.

The actual interchange circuits to be used in a particular data
communication equipment are those indicated in the appropriate CCITT
recommendation.

The usage and operational requirements of the interchange circuits
and the interaction between them are recommended in Section IV of this
Recommendation. For proper operation of the data communication equipment it is important that the guide lines in Section IV of this Recommendation are observed.

I.2   The data communication equipment may include signal convertors,
timing generators, pulse regenerators, and control circuitry, together
with equipment to provide other functions such as error control, automatic calling and automatic answering. Some of this equipment may be

198

separate intermediate equipment or it may be located in the data terminal equipment.

I.3   The range of interchange circuits defined in this recommendation is applicable, for example:

(a)   to synchronous and asynchronous data communications,

(b)   to data communication on leased line service, either 2-wire or 4-wire, either point-to-point or multipoint operation,

(c)   to data communication on switched network service, either 2-wire or 4-wire,

(d)   where short interconnection cables are used between data terminal equipment and data communication equipment. An explanation of short cable is given in Section II.

The interface between data terminal equipment and data communication equipment is located at a connector, which is the interchange point between these two classes of equipment. Separate connectors may be provided for the interchange circuits associated with the signal-conversion or similar equipment and those associated with the automatic calling equipment.

The connector(s) will not necessarily be physically attached to the data communication equipment and may be mounted in a fixed position near the data terminal equipment.

An interconnecting cable or cables will normally be provided with the data terminal equipment. The use of short cables is recommended. Their length should be limited solely by the load capacitance and other electrical characteristics specified in the relevant Recommendation on electrical characteristics.

III. DEFINITIONS OF INTERCHANGE CIRCUITS

III.1 100 series. General application

A list of these interchange circuits is presented in tabular form in Table 4.5.

Circuit 101 - Protective ground or earth

This conductor shall be electrically bonded to the machine or equipment frame. It may be further connected to external grounds as required by applicable regulations.

Circuit 102 - Signal ground or common return

This conductor establishes the signal common reference potential between

199

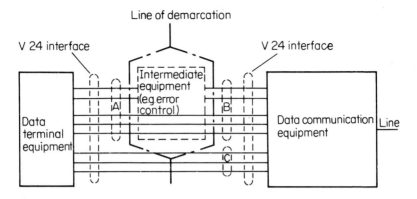

Figure A1.1.   General layout of communication equipment.
Without intermediate equipment the selection A and B
are identical.   Selection C may be a selection
specifically for automatic calling

data communication equipment and data terminal equipment. Within the
data communication equipment, this circuit shall be brought to one point,
and it shall be possible to connect this point to Circuit 101 by means
of a metallic strap within the equipment. This metallic strap can be
connected or removed at installation, as may be required to meet applicable regulations or to minimise the introduction of noise into electronic
circuitry.

Circuit 103 - Transmitted data

Direction: TO data communication equipment

The data signals originated by the data terminal equipment, to be
transmitted via the data channel to one or more remote data stations,
are transferred on this circuit to the data communication equipment.

Circuit 104 - Received data

Direction: FROM data communication equipment

The data signals generated by the data communication equipment, in
response to data channel line signals received from a remote data
station, are transferred on this circuit to the data terminal equipment.

Circuit 105 - Request to send

Direction: TO data communication equipment

Signals on this circuit control the data channel transmit function of the data communication equipment.

The ON condition causes the data communication equipment to assume the data channel transmit mode.

The OFF condition causes the data communication equipment to assume the data channel non-transmit mode, when all data transferred on Circuit 103 (Transmitted data) have been transmitted.

Circuit 106 - Ready for sending

Direction: FROM data communication equipment

Signals on this circuit indicate whether the data communication equipment is conditioned to transmit data on the data channel.

The ON condition indicates that the data communication equipment is conditioned to transmit data on the data channel.

The OFF condition indicates that the data communication equipment is not prepared to transmit data on the data channel.

Circuit 107 - Data set ready

Direction: FROM data communication equipment

Signals on this circuit indicate whether the data communication equipment is ready to operate.

The ON condition indicates that the signal-conversion or similar equipment is connected to the line and that the data communication equipment is ready to exchange further control signals with the data terminal equipment to initiate the exchange of data.

The OFF condition indicates that the data communication equipment is not ready to operate.

Circuit 108/1 - Connect data set to line

Direction: TO data communication equipment

Signals on this circuit control switching of the signal-conversion or similar equipment to or from the line.

The ON condition causes the data communication equipment to connect the signal-conversion or similar equipment to the line.

The OFF condition causes the data communication equipment to remove the signal-conversion or similar equipment from the line, when the transmission to line of all data previously transferred on Circuit 103 and/or Circuit 118 has been completed.

Circuit 108/2 - Data terminal ready

Direction: TO data communication equipment

201

Signals on this circuit control switching of the signal-conversion or similar equipment to or from the line.

The ON condition, indicating that the data terminal equipment is ready to operate, prepares the data communication equipment to connect the signal-conversion or similar equipment to the line and maintains this connection after it has been established by supplementary means.

The data terminal equipment is permitted to present the ON condition on Circuit 108/2 whenever it is ready to transmit or receive data.

The OFF condition causes the data communication equipment to remove the signal-conversion or similar equipment from the line, when the transmission to line of all data previously transferred on Circuit 103 and/or Circuit 118 has been completed.

    Circuit 109 - Data channel received line signal detector

    Direction: FROM data communication equipment

Signals on this circuit indicate whether the received data channel line signal is within appropriate limits, as specified in the relevant recommendation for data communication equipment.

The ON condition indicates that the received signal is within appropriate limits.

The OFF condition indicates that the received signal is not within appropriate limits.

    Circuit 110 - Data signal quality detector

    Direction: FROM data communication equipment

Signals on this circuit indicate whether there is a reasonable probability of an error in the data received on the data channel. The signal quality indicated conforms to the relevant data communication equipment Recommendation.

The ON condition indicates that there is no reason to believe that an error has occurred.

The OFF condition indicates that there is a reasonable probability of an error.

    Circuit 111 - Data signalling rate selector

                (data terminal equipment source)

    Direction: TO data communication equipment

Signals on this circuit are used to select one of the two data signalling rates of a dual rate synchronous data communication equipment, or to select one of the two ranges of data signalling rates of a dual range asynchronous data communication equipment.

The ON condition selects the higher rate or range of rates.

The OFF condition selects the lower rate or range of rates.

Circuit 112 - Data signalling rate selector
(data communication equipment source)
Direction: FROM data communication equipment

Signals on this circuit are used to select one of the two data signalling rates or ranges of rates in the data terminal equipment to coincide with the data signalling rate or range of rates in use in a dual rate synchronous or dual range asynchronous data communication equipment.

The ON condition selects the higher rate or range of rates.

The OFF condition selects the lower rate or range of rates.

Circuit 113 - Transmitter signal element timing
(data terminal equipment source)
Direction: TO data communication equipment

Signals on this circuit provide the data communication equipment with signal element timing information.

The condition on this circuit shall be ON and OFF for nominally equal periods of time, and the transition from ON to OFF condition shall nominally indicate the centre of each signal element on Circuit 103 (Transmitted data).

Circuit 114 - Transmitter signal element timing
(data communication equipment source)
Direction: FROM data communication equipment

Signals on this circuit provide the data terminal equipment with signal element timing information.

The condition on this circuit shall be ON and OFF for nominally equal periods of time. The data terminal equipment shall present a data signal on Circuit 103 (Transmitted data) in which the transitions between signal elements nominally occur at the time of the transitions from OFF to ON condition of Circuit 114.

Circuit 115 - Receiver signal element timing
(data communication equipment source)
Direction: FROM data communication equipment

Signals on this circuit provide the data terminal equipment with signal element timing information.

The condition of this circuit shall be ON and OFF for nominally equal periods of time, and a transition fron ON to OFF condition shall nominally indicate the centre of each signal element on Circuit 104 (Received data).

Circuit 116 - Select standby
Direction: TO data communication equipment

Signals on this circuit are used to select the normal or standby facilities, such as signal convertors and communication channels.
The ON condition selects the standby mode of operation, causing the data communication equipment to replace predetermined facilities by their reserves.
The OFF condition causes the data communication equipment to replace the standby facilities by the normal. The OFF condition on this circuit shall be maintained whenever the standby facilities are not required for use.

Circuit 117 - Standby indicator
Direction: FROM data communication equipment

Signals on this circuit indicate whether the data communication equipment is conditioned to operate in its standby mode with the predetermined facilities replaced by their reserves.
The ON condition indicates that the data communication equipment is conditioned to operate in its standby mode.
The OFF condition indicates that the data communication equipment is conditioned to operate in its normal mode.

Circuit 118 - Transmitted backward channel data
Direction: TO data communication equipment

This circuit is equivalent to Circuit 103 (Transmitted data) except that it is used to transmit data via the backward channel.

Circuit 119 - Received backward channel data
Direction: FROM data communication equipment

This circuit is equivalent to Circuit 104 (Received data), except that it is used for data received on the backward channel.

Circuit 120 - Transmit backward channel line signal
Direction: TO data communication equipment

This circuit is equivalent to Circuit 105 (Request to send), except that it is used to control the backward channel transmit function of the data communication equipment.

The ON condition causes the data communication equipment to assume the backward channel transmit mode.

The OFF condition causes the data communication equipment to assume the backward channel non-transmit mode, when all data transferred on Circuit 118 (Transmitted backward channel data) have been transmitted to line.

Circuit 121 - Backward channel ready
Direction: FROM data communication equipment

This circuit is equivalent to Circuit 106 (Ready for sending), except that it is used to indicate whether the data communication equipment is conditioned to transmit data on the backward channel.

The ON condition indicates that the data communication equipment is conditioned to transmit data on the backward channel.

The OFF condition indicates that the data communication equipment is not conditioned to transmit data on the backward channel.

Circuit 122 - Backward channel received line signal detector
Direction: FROM data communication equipment

This circuit is equivalent to Circuit 109 (Data channel received line signal detector), except that it is used to indicate whether the received backward channel line signal is within appropriate limits, as specified in the relevant recommendation for data communication equipment.

Circuit 123 - Backward channel signal quality detector
Direction: FROM data communication equipment

This circuit is equivalent to Circuit 110 (Data signal quality detector), except that it is used to indicate the signal quality of the received backward channel line signal.

Circuit 124 - Select frequency groups
Direction: TO data communication equipment

Signals on this circuit are used to select the desired frequency groups available in the data communication equipment.

The ON condition causes the data communication equipment to use all frequency groups to represent data signals.

The OFF condition causes the data communication equipment to use a specified reduced number of frequency groups to represent data signals.

Circuit 125 - Calling indicator
Direction: FROM data communication equipment

Signals on this circuit indicate whether a calling signal is being received by the data communication equipment.
The ON condition indicates that a calling signal is being received.
The OFF condition indicates that no calling signal is being received, and this condition may also appear during interruptions of a pulse modulated calling signal.

Circuit 126 - Select transmit frequency
Direction: TO data communication equipment

Signals on this circuit are used to select the required transmit frequency of the data communication equipment.
The ON condition selects the higher transmit frequency.
The OFF condition selects the lower transmit frequency.

Circuit 127 - Select receive frequency
Direction: TO data communication equipment

Signals on this circuit are used to select the required receive frequency of the data communication equipment.
The ON condition selects the lower receive frequency.
The OFF condition selects the higher receive frequency.

Circuit 128 - Receiver signal element timing
Direction: TO data communication equipment

Signals on this circuit provide the data communication equipment with signal element timing information.
The condition on this circuit shall be ON and OFF for nominally equal periods of time. The data communication equipment shall present a data signal on Circuit 104 (Received data) in which the transitions between signal elements nominally occur at the time of the transitions from OFF to ON condition of the signal on Circuit 128.

Circuit 129 - Request to receive
Direction: TO data communication equipment

Signals on this circuit are used to control the receive function of the data communication equipment.
The ON condition causes the data communication equipment to assume the receive mode.
The OFF condition causes the data communication equipment to assume the non-receive mode.

Circuit 130 - Transmit backward tone

Direction: TO data communication equipment

Signals on this circuit control the transmission of a backward channel tone.

The ON condition causes the data communication equipment to transmit a backward channel tone.

The OFF condition causes the data communication equipment to stop the transmission of a backward channel tone.

Circuit 131 - Received character timing

Direction: FROM data communication equipment

Signals on this circuit provide the data terminal equipment with character timing information, as specified in the relevant recommendation for data communication equipment.

Circuit 132 - Return to non-data mode

Direction: TO data communication equipment

Signals on this circuit are used to restore the non-data mode provided with the data communication equipment, without releasing the line connection to the remote station.

The ON condition causes the data communication equipment to restore the non-data mode. When the non-data mode has been established, this circuit must be turned OFF.

Circuit 133 - Ready for receiving

Direction: TO data communication equipment

Signals on this circuit control the transfer of data on Circuit 104 (Received data), indicating whether the data terminal equipment is capable of accepting a given amount of data (e.g. a block of data), specified in the appropriate recommendation for intermediate equipment, for example, error control equipment.

The ON condition must be maintained whenever the data terminal equipment is capable of accepting data, and causes the intermediate equipment to transfer the received data to the data terminal equipment.

The OFF condition indicates that the data terminal equipment is not able to accept data, and causes the intermediate equipment to retain the data.

Circuit 134 - Received data present

Direction: FROM data communication equipment

207

Signals on this circuit are used to separate information messages from supervisory messages, transferred on Circuit 104 (Received data), as specified in the appropriate Recommendation for intermediate equipment, e.g. error control equipment.
The ON condition indicates the data which represent information messages. The OFF condition shall be maintained at all other times.

Circuit 191 - Transmitted voice answer
Direction: TO data communication equipment

Signals generated by a voice enswer unit in the data terminal equipment are transferred on this circuit to the data communication equipment. The electrical characteristics of this analogue interchange circuit are part of the appropriate data communication equipment Recommendation.

Circuit 192 - Received voice answer
Direction: FROM data communication equipment

Received voice signals, generated by a voice answering unit at the remote data terminal, are transferred on this circuit to the data terminal equipment.
The electrical characteristics of this analogue interchange circuit are part of the appropriate data communication equipment Recommendation.

APPENDIX 2

(a) CCITT Draft Recommendation X.20

Many data terminal equipments are in use which are equipped with interfaces recommended for existing networks such as Recommendation V.21 for duplex working over telephone networks. For a period of time data networks will also provide similar interfaces for start/stop operation. For the long term a new simpler interface is recommended and described below.

I. SCOPE

I.1 This recommendation applies to the interconnecting circuits being called interchange circuits, between Data Terminal Equipment (DTE) and Data Circuit-Terminating Equipments (DCE) for the transfer of binary data and control signals.

I.2 This DCE provides all signal conversions between the DTE and the data circuit. It may or may not be a specific or separate piece of equipment.

I.3 The interchange circuits defined in this Recommendation are applicable to DTE of the user-classes 1 and 2 (see Recommendation X.1) where short interconnecting cables are used between the DTE and the DCE (*see* Section 4).

II. LINE OF DEMARCATION

The interface between DTE and DCE is located at a connector which is the interchange point between these two classes of equipment.

An interconnecting cable or cables will normally be provided with the data terminal equipment. The use of short cables is recommended with the length solely limited by the load capacitance and other electrical characteristics, specified in Section 4.

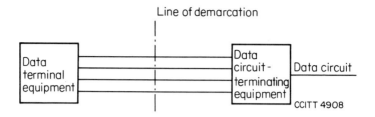

Line of demarcation

CCITT 4908

Figure A2(a).1. Layout of data terminal equipment and data
circuit terminating equipment

III. DEFINITIONS OF INTERCHANGE CIRCUITS

General application

A list of these interchange circuits is presented in tabular form
in Table A2(a).1.

Circuit 101 - Protective ground or earth

This conductor shall be electrically bonded to the machine or equipment
frame. It may be further connected to external grounds as required by
applicable regulations.

Circuit 102A - Signal ground or common return

This conductor establishes the common reference potential for all interchange circuits, except circuit 101 (protective ground or earth). Within
the data circuit terminating equipment, this circuit shall be brought
to one point, and it shall be possible to connect this point to circuit -
protective ground or earth by means of a wire strap inside the equipment.

Table A2(a).1. *Interchange circuits*

Interchange circuit number	Interchange circuit name	Ground	Data	
			to DCE	from DCE
101	Protective ground or earth	x		
102A	Signal ground or common return	x		
103A	Transmitted data		x	
104A	Received data			x

210

This wire strap can be connected or removed at installation, as may be required to meet applicable regulations or to minimise the introduction or noise into electronic circuitry.

Circuit 103A - Transmitted data
Direction: TO data circuit-terminating equipment

The data signals originated by the data terminal equipment to be transmitted via the data channel to one or more remote data stations are passed on this circuit to the data circuit-terminating equipment. Moreover, all data signals produced by the data terminal equipment during the call establishment and the disconnection and being required by the network to establish and clear connections are transmitted via this circuit. The operational conditions indicated to the data network are also included (*see* Section 5).

During an established connection and the setting-up phase of a call as well as during all intervals between the signals, the DTE shall keep the circuit "transmitted data" in Z-polarity.

Circuit 104A - Received data
Direction: FROM data circuit-terminating equipment

The data signals generated by a remote DTE and transmitted via the data network are passed on this circuit to the DTE.

Furthermore, all data signals generated by the data network during call establishment and the clearing and being required by the data terminal equipment to establish and clear connections are transmitted via this circuit.

(b) CCITT Draft Recommendation X.21

SCOPE

This recommendation is the basis of and defines the important parameters for a general-purpose interface for synchronous operation on public data networks.

1. INTERCHANGE CIRCUITS USED

Protective ground or earth
Signal ground or common return
Transmit data
Receive data
Control DTE source
Control DCE source
Signal element timing DCE source
Frame timing DCE source (where provided)

Additional study is required to prepare definitions of these circuits where these are not given in Recommendation V.24.

2. INTERFACE SIGNALLING SCHEME

The procedures and the conditions on the interchange circuits (except timing circuits) for various stages in the progress of a call are given in Table A2(b).1. The precise timing relationships between the changes of state on the various interchange circuits is not yet defined and is subject to further study.

Table A2(b).1. *Interface signalling scheme*

Call phase	DTE	Event	Interchange circuits			
			Transmitted data	Received data	Control DTE source	Control DCE source
Establishment	Calling	Free line	0	0	OFF	OFF
		Call request	1	0	ON	OFF
		Proceed to select	1	Ch	ON	OFF
		Selection signals	Ch	1	ON	OFF
		Selection acknowledgement	1	Ch	ON	OFF
		Waiting	1	1	ON	OFF
		Connect through or call progress signals	1	Ch	ON	OFF
		Data transfer	DATA	DATA	ON	OFF
	Called	Free line	0	0	OFF	OFF
		Incoming call	0	1	OFF	OFF
		Call confirmation	Ch	1	ON	OFF
		Connect through	1	Ch	ON	OFF
		Data transfer	DATA	DATA	ON	ON
DATA	BOTH		DATA	DATA	ON	ON
Disconnection	Clearing	Data transfer	DATA	DATA	ON	ON
		Clear request	0	DATA	OFF	ON
		Clear confirmation	0	0	OFF	OFF
		Free line	0	0	OFF	OFF
	Cleared	Data transfer	DATA	DATA	ON	ON
		Clear indication	DATA	0	ON	OFF
		Clear confirmation	0	0	OFF	OFF
		Free line	0	0	OFF	OFF
Control signalling after entering data phase		Data transfer	DATA	DATA	ON	ON
		Control request	Ch	DATA	OFF	ON
		Control response	1	Ch	ON	OFF
		Continue data	DATA	DATA	ON	ON
	Other station		To be defined			

213

Data - information generated by the DTE and can be any bit sequence.

States of interchange circuits

0	-	Continuous binary 0
1	-	Continuous binary 1
ON	-	Continuous ON condition (binary 0 or + ve)
OFF	-	Continuous OFF condition (binary 1 or - ve)
Ch	-	Characters used for all progressing, selection and control signalling selected from International Alphabet No. 5 to Recommendations V.3 and V.4 (7 bits + odd parity). The choice of characters is not yet specified.

Signal element timing is provided continuously by the DCE

Frame timing is provided continuously by the DCE where this is required by the national network. (*see* Section 3).

Selection address will be terminated by an end of selection character.

Data phase commences when the control DCE source interchange circuit turns ON and terminates when this circuit turns OFF.

Head-on collision may be detected by DTE as Proceed to Select will be a different character from incoming call. DTE may decide to accept incoming call by returning call confirmation character instead of selection signals. If call confirmation is not sent by DTE then data switch will return busy to original caller and attempt to respond to new call demand. If the data switch is unable to proceed with call then it will send clear. Some administrations may find it an advantage as an interim message (except on user class of service 6) to use the all 1's condition as the proceed to select signal leaving the resolution of collision entirely to the switch.

Connect-through

The connect-through-signal is to be generated by the network and when received by the DTEs data transmission and reception can commence. This signal will indicate that all bits sent by either terminal after the connect-through indication is received shall be delivered to the corresponding terminal after the receipt of the connect-through signal at that corresponding terminal.

Note: At the local station, the connect-through indication may be followed by either bits originated in the distant DTE or in the network. If generated in the network, the maximum duration and pattern of these bits shall be specified after further study.

Clearing

Data bits delivered to the network before the clearing signal is applied from the same DTE must be delivered to the distant DTE before the clear signal arrives at that DTE. This may require safeguards in the signalling system, e.g. centralised system.

Note: During the clear-down process, bits generated by the network may be received by the DTEs. The maximum duration and pattern of such bits shall be specified after further study.

Remote terminal identification if provided by the network will occur before the connect-through-signal.

3. CHARACTER ALIGNMENT

Two methods of providing character alignment between the DTE and the data network are defined:

(a)   No frame timing interchange circuit is provided and all control character sequences to and from the network are preceded by "n" SYN characters, where the number "n" is left for further study.

(b)   A frame timing interchange circuit is provided. This circuit will define continuous 24 bit sequences, i.e. three International Alphabet No. 5 characters. (Further study is required to determine if an 8 bit sequence is possible.) All control character sequences to and from the network shall be properly aligned with the indications on the frame timing circuit. SYN characters are not required and may not be provided by the network or by the DTE.

Note 1 Alphabet for control signalling between DTE and a data network

An agreed coded character set is necessary to permit exchange of control information both for call set up and call progress purposes. This is solely for control signalling between DTE and the network and may not be applicable for signalling between data signalling exchanges.

International Alphabet No. 5 has already been standardised and is therefore an attractive solution since its use avoids the work involved in developing a new alphabet. However, the use of this alphabet has been criticised on the grounds that the number of code combinations

215

exceeds those required for network control purposes. Examination of the structure of the code table in Recommendation V.3 shows that the allocation of characters to the various columns is such that various network proposals require characters from at least 5 columns e.g. alpha characters from columns 4 and 5, numericals from column 3 and control characters from columns 0 and 1. A subset of International Alphabet No. 5 is not therefore readily possible for all purposes. The use of International Alphabet No. 5 in total permits characters to be chosen which are most appropriate for the various functions. It is not expected that all 128 code combinations will be necessary for data network control signalling and indeed may not be suitable, e.g. those left for national options.

In summary the use of International Alphabet No. 5 gives the needed flexibility without the need for a new standard.

Note 2

A basic or simple binary interface with minimum or no logic in the NTU is the subject of further study.

Note 3

Interfaces similar to those in the V series recommendations may be provided by some administrations.

APPENDIX 3
SHORT GLOSSARY

Address: In data communications this is normally the identifying character(s) for a terminal on a multidropped line.

Alternate routing: On important circuits the Post Office are often able to arrange alternate routing of backup lines as a safety measure. Unfortunately, the local ends (which are most vulnerable) almost invariably go through the same cable, thereby minimising the benefit of such an arrangement.

Amplitude modulation: *see* Chapter 4

ASCII: American Standard Code for information Interchange. A 7 or 8 bit code for data transmission established by the American National Standards Institute. *see* Chapter 5.

Asynchronous transmission: Sometimes called 'start-stop'. *see* Chapter 4.

Auto-dialling: The automatic initiation of calls on the public (telegraph or telephone) networks.

Bandwidth: The range of frequencies on a circuit available for transmission.

Baud: Unit of signalling speed. *see* Chapter 4.

Bit rate: The speed at which bits are transmitted. This is not necessarily the same as baud rate. *see* Chapter 4.

Carrier: Continuous-frequency signal which can be modulated to carry data.

Circuits: *see* Chapter 3.

Data Set: American name for a modem (*not* an OS/360 file). IBM sometimes use 'line adapter' to refer to modems.

Demodulation: Opposite of 'modulation'. *see* Chapter 4.

Dial-up: The use of a dial to initiate connections on switched telegraph or telephone networks.

Duplex transmission: Transmission of data in both directions simultaneously (i.e. full duplex). *see* Chapter 4.

Duplexing: The use of duplicated system components, one acting as standby for the other.

Echoplexing: A system whereby characters (sometimes messages) are printed or displayed back at the originating terminal for comparison with the original for checking purposes.

Exchange: A switching-point in a telephone or telegraph network. May belong to the Post Office or be a private exchange. See PBX and PABX.

Facsimile: A system for transmission of documents.

Fail softly: An arrangement whereby the failure of system components cause a gradual degradation of service to the user but not a complete failure of the system.

FDX: Full-duplex.

FDM: Frequency Division Multiplexing. *see* Chapters 4 and 7.

Firmware: See 'Microprogram'

Four-Wire circuit: A circuit consisting of a combination of two standard 'pairs' used for speech.

Frequency modulation: *see* Chapter 4.

HDX: Half-duplex. Transmission of data in both directions possible but in one direction only at any one time.

Hertz (Hz): Cycles per second.

In-House: A system restricted to one building, factory or other location such that Post Office lines are not required.

ITU: International Telecommunications Union. The telecommunications agency of United Nations.

Local End: The part of a telephone line running between the user's office and local exchange.

Local Exchange: The Post Office switching centre to which subscriber's lines are attached. There are higher levels of exchanges linking LEs called Group Switching Centres and Zone Switching Centres.

Message Switching: A system whereby a message is received from one terminal and then transmitted on to another (generally without any processing taking place).

Micro-program: The non-dynamic implementation of a 'software-like' series of commands in a hardware component, thus enabling that component to perform different functions in different situations according to its initial programming.

Modem: 'Modulator-Demodulator'. *see* Chapter 4.

Modulation   *see* Chapter 4.

Multidrop line: The sharing of a line between a number of terminals.

Multiplexing: The sharing of a line between a number of terminals by splitting the frequency band or by allocation time-slots. *see* Chapter 7.

Noise: Random signals which disturb transmission on lines and cause errors.

Off line: Not connected to the computer.

On line: Connected to the computer, either directly to the I/O channel or over a telecommunications link.

PABX: Private Automatic Branch Exchange. A privately owned telephone exchange which permits the automatic establishment of a link between internal extensions and between extensions and the public telephone network.

PBX: Private Branch Exchange. As for PABX but not automatic, i.e. connections effected by a switchboard operator.

Phase modulation: *see* Chapter 4.

Polling: A method of controlling the conversation between the computer and the terminals. *see* Chapter 5.

Private line: A line leased from the Post Office for the exclusive use of the leasee.

Public Switched Network (PSN):   A service which provides circuit switching to a large number of independent users.

Pushbutton dialling: Not yet available in the U.K. (except on private exchanges). A method of connecting circuits using combinations of tones rather than series of pulses.

Real Time: Generally used to mean 'fast response'. Originally meant a system which accepted signals from an environment and could process and return signals fast enough to be able to control that environment.

Redundancy checking: The insertion of data (in addition to information bits) which can be used to check the accuracy of data to be transmitted (or stored). Parity checks are an example. *see* Chapter 5.

Simplex line: Data transmission possible in one direction only. *see* Chapter 4.

Start-stop transmission: Asynchronous transmission. *see* Chapter 4.

Store-and-forward: A technique used in a network to concentrate lines. *see* Chapter 7.

Synchronous transmission: *see* Chapter 4.

Telex Service: The switched public telegraph service. *see* Chapters 1 and 10.

Terminal: *see* Chapter 6.

Time division multiplexing (TDM): *see* Chapter 7.

Wideband: Communications channels having a wider bandwidth than
that used for normal speech circuits, very high speed
(e.g. 48k bits/sec) transmission. (Broadband in USA).

Index